"I just finished reading *Stakes Is High*. My h⟨ narrative of violence against black and brow States finds its way into homes, churches, schools, and offices of public servants across this nation. I will recommend it to the faculty, staff, and students of the institution that I lead, Duke Divinity School. Michael Waters' straightforward account of brutality begins with slavery and leads us forward to our own day in which killings are repeated endlessly on social media. Waters speaks with prophetic authority, calling all of us to the way of justice and peace."
— Elaine A. Heath, Dean, Duke Divinity School

"Timely and important. Too often these words are used for books simply well written; not so here. *Stakes Is High* is the rare book that brings a keen theological eye to contemporary events. In the midst of what has been one of the most important movements for human dignity, Black Lives Matter, in recent decades, hearing the voice of emerging Christian leadership dedicated to both chronicling the moment and changing the world is vital! The book is a resource for practitioners of public ministry and those of us dedicated to their preparation."
— Stephen G. Ray Jr., Fisher Professor of Theology,
　Garrett-Evangelical Theological Seminary

"Through raw emotion and critical analysis, *Stakes Is High* grapples with the race matters plaguing America. Shifting us away from sound bites, Waters takes us on a journey that is deeply historical, theological, cultural, and personal. In the end, we are challenged to view the complexities of the black experience in ways that are both familiar and fresh."
— Rahiel Tesfamariam, Founder/Publisher of *Urban Cusp*

"Captivating and persuasive, *Stakes Is High* offers a poignant reflection on the social, political, and theological situations of Black people in America. With great skill, Waters reveals the contradictions in the American system of justice as well as the progress people of faith have made with prophetic resistance. This critical time in the Black freedom struggle requires revolutionary movements that dismantle systems of oppression and empower the next generation of change makers – Waters offers a personal account of leading in such a movement."
— Stephen A. Green, National Director, NAACP Youth
　and College Division

"Waters challenges us to consider the question 'How often must we drink from this bitter well? of racism in America.' His use of historical narratives juxtaposed with contemporary illustrations gives the reader a sense of this long arc of injustice. Waters mixes the names of familiar and lesser known people who have found themselves on the underside of this arc and challenges us to think critically and creatively about next steps toward liberty and justice for all."
— Leah Gunning Francis, Christian Theological Seminary, author
   of *Ferguson and Faith*

"No one will remain unaffected as Michael Waters masterfully tells the stories of the struggle and gives powerful evidence for the hope that things are about to change."
— Joerg Rieger, Vanderbilt University, author of
   Unified We Are a Force

"Michael Waters personifies the truthful image of a powerful, young, Black pastor/preacher/lecturer, raw cultural writer, boots on the ground, social justice advocate, and true lover of hip-hop music. *Stakes Is High* is powerful and thought-provoking."
— Sharon Risher, Chaplain, gun law reform advocate,
   daughter of Emanuel 9 martyr

"In *Stakes Is High* Dr. Waters shares some of his most thought-provoking writings on race relations in the United States. Part theology/part commentary this book has a wide reach and relevance from seminaries to academic classrooms to book clubs. Dr. Waters will challenge you, inspire you, and make you question your own thoughts about the state of the nation."
— John Thomas III, Editor, *The Christian Recorder* and
   General Officer of the African Methodist Episcopal Church

STAKES IS
HIGH

**RACE, FAITH,
AND HOPE
FOR AMERICA**

MICHAEL W. WATERS

FOREWORD BY VASHTI MURPHY MCKENZIE

**chalice
press**

Saint Louis, Missouri

An imprint of Christian Board of Publication

ChalicePress.com

Print: 9780827235403   EPUB: 9780827235410
EPDF: 9780827235427

Printed in the USA.

For my mother, the Reverend B. Williams Waters,
who taught me to love God, to love all God's people, and in
defiance of the deep-seated racism in our society,
to love myself.
I love you!

And to the martyrs of the Mother Emanuel A.M.E.
Church massacre in Charleston, South Carolina:
May you continue to rest in the presence of God;
and on that great and holy day,
may we take flight together as with the wings of eagles.
We will never forget you!

CONTENTS

Series Foreword

Cultivating Faithful, Wise, and Courageous Leaders for the Church and Academy

Welcome to a conversation at the intersection of young adults, faith, and leadership. The Forum for Theological Exploration (FTE) is a leadership incubator that inspires diverse young people to make a difference in the world through Christian communities. This series, published in partnership with Chalice Press, reimagines Christian leadership and creates innovative approaches to ministry and scholarship from diverse contexts.

These books are written by and for a growing network of:

- Partners seeking to cultivate the Christian leaders, pastors, and theological educators needed to renew and respond to a changing church.

- Young leaders exploring alternative paths to ministry and following traditional ways of serving the common good —both inside and beyond "the walls" of the church and theological academy.

- Christian leaders developing new ways to awaken the search for meaning and purpose in young adults who are inspired to shape the future.

- Members of faith communities creating innovative solutions to address the needs of their congregations, institutions, and the broader community.

This series offers an opportunity to discover what FTE is learning, widen the circle of conversation, and share ideas FTE believes are necessary for faith communities to shape a more hopeful future. Authors' expressed ideas and opinions in this series are their own and do not necessarily reflect the views of FTE.

Thank you for joining us!

Dori Baker, Series Editor

Stephen Lewis, FTE President

FOREWORD

"If you get rid of unfair practices, quit blaming victims, quit gossiping about other people's sins, if you are generous with the hungry and start giving yourselves to the down-and-out, your lives will begin to glow in the darkness, your shadowed lives will be bathed in sunlight. I will always show you where to go. I'll give you a full life in the emptiest of places." —Isaiah 58:9–12 (MSG)

"Action without reflection is mere activism and reflection without action is pure verbalism."
—Paulo Freire

I wrote a letter to my toddler granddaughter recently expressing my hopes for her future in America. My hope was that she will inherit a United States that wasn't so divided. We are a nation of *"...huddled masses yearning to breathe free..."* and at the same time a nation that supports violent, racist, misogynist rhetoric and actions. We are *"...the land of the free and the home of the brave!"* and a nation that applauds trash-talk, name calling, and uncivil discourse. We are a nation of diverse races, religions, and ethnic origins seeking inclusivity in an America that *"...rings with the harmony of liberty..."* and a nation with an ugly undercarriage of anger, fear, and hate.

Was *"...liberty and justice for all"* too much to hope for?

The great poet Langston Hughes asked questions of his Harlem Renaissance audience/20th-century America. "What happens to a dream deferred? Does it dry up like a raisin in the sun?" Playwright Lorraine Hansberry fleshed out an answer in her award winning play *A Raisin in the Sun*. Marvin Gaye asked "What's going on?" in his seminal song of protest. Pulitzer Prize playwright August

Wilson snapchats a response with his *The Century Cycle* plays chronicling the stresses and struggles of 20th-century African Americans.

Gil Scott-Heron said, "The Revolution will not be televised" while the Winans sang, "It's time, time to make a change, we are the people who can do it."

An African American spiritual also asked questions, four to be exact:

> *Were you there when they crucified my Lord? Were you there when they nailed him to the tree? Were you there when they pierced him in the side? Were you there when the sun refused to shine? Sometimes it causes me to tremble.*

This series of questions were not meant to be taken literally. The questions were meant to challenge the listener to remember. It is the kind of remembering that allows the past to reemerge with a fresh impact upon the present. It is like a form of anamnesis, a Greek word that calls the community of listeners to make what happened in the past a part of their present story. It is recalling of the sacrifice of Jesus Christ, and the "Do this in remembrance of me." (Luke 22/ 1 Corinthians 11:23–26). It is a call to go from passive listening to active engagement.

James Cones writes in *The Cross and The Lynching Tree* that the paradox of a crucified Jesus Christ is the heart of the Christian story. It makes no rational or spiritual sense to say that hope came out of a place called Golgotha. The broken body, shed blood on a cross, and the empty tomb invert the world's value system. The Christian story says that hope comes by way of what looks like a defeat. It says to the believer that God can make a way out of no way. It says that death and suffering do not have the last word.

When our ancestors sang, "Were you there" it helped them to remember that although there was an ancient public spectacle accompanied by torture and shame, eternal life came out of death. They were just as valuable to God as any other human being. They too were a part of the "Whosoever" (John 3:16, KJV). There was still hope in their present reality.

In our 21st-century recalling of "Were you there when..." God radically altered social, political, and religious realities on a cross and from an empty tomb, we now have an opportunity to remember again how triumph came out of tragedy. It helps us to tread the dangerous paths from passive listening to active engagement when we are faced with the present social, political, and religious realities from the horrific events in Dallas, Texas, New York City, Ferguson, Missouri, Baltimore, Maryland, Florida. *"It causes me to tremble, tremble, tremble."*

The Rev. Dr. Michael W. Waters in *Stakes Is High* is the prophetic griot who tells the stories that upset our sensibilities. He asks the hard questions that can make you uncomfortable. He opens the door exposing our political, social, and religious realities so that the reader can begin the journey from passivity to active engagement.

In the same way that our ancestors sang, "Were you there?" Waters asks were you there when Michael Brown was shot in the middle of the street? Were you there when Freddie Gray was put in the back of the police van? Were you there when Sandra Bland was put in jail or when a bikini-clad teenager was slammed to the ground? Were you there in Bible study at Mother Emanuel A.M.E. Church when the pastor and eight members were murdered?

It is a call to remember beyond the hashtags of social media. Waters is asking us to reflect upon what has happened in the past and make it a part of our present day activism. Whatever shape or form of activism—the streets, halls of congress, city hall or the courts, business or education, pulpit or pew—as Paulo Freire states, "Action without reflection is mere activism and reflection without action is pure verbalism."

Waters is a part of the emerging new generation of prophetic activists. He utilizes his gifts to preach, pray, march, rally, and speak truth to power. He and his family were there when five Dallas police officers tragically lost their lives at the end of a peaceful demonstration after the deaths of Alton Sterling and Philando Castile.

The embers of anger and frustration still burn brightly because you can love and hug your children in the morning not sure what will happen to them during the day. You say goodbye before school or work praying that everyone will come home alive. In America we wear violence like a loose garment that we fail to take off at the end of the day. Senseless acts of violence are unacceptable, the senseless acts of violence against unarmed men and women and against those who are sworn to protect and serve.

Stakes Is High reminds us that it is past time for a new generation of prophets to roll back the stone from the tomb of a radically divided existence to set free the gallant aspirations and noble commitments of the Declaration of Independence. It is past time for a new generation of trustees who will work to protect and preserve our right to free press, free religion, free speech, and free assembly. It's past time to "get rid of unfair practices, quit blaming victims, quit gossiping about other people's sins and become generous with the hungry and give yourselves to the down-and-out so that your lives will begin to glow in the darkness, your shadowed lives will be bathed in sunlight. You will rebuild ancient ruins, repair broken walls, and restore the streets. God will always show you where to go. God will give you a full life in the emptiest of places" (Isaiah 58:9–12, MSG).

Vashti Murphy McKenzie,
117th elected and consecrated bishop of
the African Methodist Episcopal Church
Dallas, Texas
December, 2016

Introduction

I have long felt that by virtue of the year and month of my birth, I occupy a unique space in time and in the history of America. I am too young to claim the '70s as the decade of my childhood, but I am young enough to have had some formative childhood experiences to transpire in the early '90s. I am technically a member of Generation X, but just by a few months. I am old enough to have been alive when President Jimmy Carter was in office, yet young enough to have no memory of his service. President Ronald Reagan was the first sitting president I knew, and the Challenger explosion is the first national tragedy of my recollection.

Consequently my experience has always been dualistic, part Generation X and part Millennial, which are vastly different experiences. Another way of conceiving this unique space in time is as a member of both the first and second generations of hip hop. It is in and through this experience that I first discerned—at the age of 11—the call to ministry.

I am a member of a family deeply rooted in faith. My great-grandmother, the Reverend Willie B. Williams, was one of the first women to be ordained in the African Methodist Episcopal Church in the State of Texas. She was also one of the first women to pastor a congregation in the state. Roberson Chapel A.M.E. Church in McGregor, Texas, was founded in my great-great-grandmother Missouri Green's home in 1905. My great-great-great grandfather, the Reverend William Leake, was a circuit-riding preacher, one of four who founded Paul Quinn College in 1872, the oldest historically Black college west of the Mississippi River. My mother, the Reverend Brenda Williams Waters, and my father, the Reverend Kenneth L. Waters, Ph.D., are both ordained ministers, my father, one of a select few Black* Americans to hold an earned doctorate in New Testament Studies.[1]

My family is also filled with educators, entrepreneurs, active laypersons in God's church, artists, and the civically and socially engaged. My grandfather's participation in the Falls County NAACP once earned him a personal home visit from the Grand Dragon of the Ku Klux Klan. My late grandfather, Mr. Bishop W. Williams—the greatest man I have ever known—invited the Klansman in for coffee and assured him that nothing would stop my grandfather from his pursuits of justice. In my family, faith, service, and justice have always been married together. I was inspired early in life to join and continue my family's legacy of the same in and to my own generation.

Still, while my family of origin played a significant role in shaping my understanding of mission, service, and call, as did my upbringing as part of the A.M.E. Church, a denomination birthed two centuries ago out of the struggle for racial justice in America, hip hop played an indelible role as well. Through the speakers of my Boombox and through headphones attached to my CD Discman as a youth, urban prophets ministered to me daily— their voices of lament and pain, too, crying out for justice. One particular offering that greatly shaped the lens through which I viewed society was seminal hip hop group De La Soul's 1996 offering "Stakes Is High."

On the mesmerizing title track produced by the late and legendary J Dilla (listed as Jay Dee on the song credits), De La Soul exchanges bars critiquing the state of segments of hip hop culture, especially the rampant materialism and promotion of violence that had begun to dominate commercial rap. In one particular verse, band member Dave exclaims, "I'm sick of talkin' about blunts / Sick of Versace glasses / Sick of slang / ...Sick of name brand clothes." However, it is Dave's band member Posdnuos who offers several devastating lines regarding his observations concerning the racial politics of America. Declaring that "Every word I say should be a hip hop quotable," Posdnuos cements the following laments in rhyme:

---

* The B in *Black* is capitalized throughout the book. For more about the decision to capitalize, see nytimes.com/2014/11/19/opinion/the-case-for-black-with-a-capital-b.html?_r=0 .

"I gets down like brothers are found ducking from bullets/ Gun control means using both hands in my land/ Where it's all about the cautious livin'."

"Let me tell you what it's all about/ A skin not considered equal/ A meteor has more right than my people."

"Neighborhoods are now hoods 'cause nobody's neighbors/ Just animals surviving with that animal behavior."

"Experiments when needles and skin connect/ No wonder where we live is called the projects."²

A sense of urgency is present in each line of "Stakes Is High." A pulsating beat adds to this sense of urgency as De La Soul seeks to awaken the masses from their slumber concerning critical matters of race in our nation. The chorus offers no reprieve from the urgency of the verses, just the repeated proclamation that "Stakes is high/ Y'all know them stakes is high."

Fifteen years ago, during my first year in seminary, I was introduced to a paper on theology and hip hop culture in Dr. Harold J. Recinos's The Church in Its Social Context course at the Perkins School of Theology at Southern Methodist University in Dallas, Texas. I would later offer a classroom presentation based on my engagement with the text. The total experience served to enlighten me further as to the power of hip hop culture and hip hop lyricism to inspire change and movements for justice, a topic that would inspire my doctoral dissertation a decade later at Perkins.

Fast forward 12 years from the release of the song "Stakes Is High." In the same month that President Barack Obama was elected as the first bi-racial, self-identifying Black president in American history, I was appointed by my bishop to establish the first successful African Methodist Episcopal church plant, Joy Tabernacle A.M.E. Church, in over four decades in Dallas, the nation's ninth largest city in the nation's second-fastest-growing region. I had previously been appointed to serve three historic congregations in rural, peri-urban, and urban contexts, as well as be the dean of chapel at Paul Quinn College. Yet I was excited to be a part of something new, a church that could offer a wholly

21st–century witness to the opportunities and challenges facing our nation and our community.

In 2008, much of the country was swept away with proclamations of hope. Following the terrorist attacks of September 11, 2001, the subsequent fighting of two wars simultaneously in Iraq and Afghanistan, Hurricane Katrina (America's worst natural disaster aided by historically and environmentally racist policies), and the Great Recession, the nation was anxious to experience hope anew. Surely the election of a Black president marked a new day in our nation, especially a nation that has experienced the pains of racial strife since its inception.

The flames of this hope, a hope built on the falsified proclamation that America was now a post-racial society, were soon diminished. During President Obama's first months in office, threats against the president increased by 400% with the United States Secret Service managing 30 potential death threats to President Obama every day.[3] President Obama will end two terms in office as the most threatened president in American history.[4]

During the Obama era, the membership of hate groups in America skyrocketed, including a resurgence of the Ku Klux Klan. During the Obama era, the purchase of firearms exploded nationally. Throughout his presidency, President Obama and his family have been treated with contempt by both the media and by members of Congress in ways that further attest to the racial tension of this era. Numerous public officials have been forced to resign over eight years for racially-charged statements made against the Obamas, including disturbing statements made concerning their two daughters.

The years encompassing President Obama's service have also witnessed public outcries against police brutality and the frequent killing of unarmed Black women, children, and men. In the Obama era, grand juries have also frequently failed to indict police officers in these cases. In the Obama era, we have witnessed an increase in wealth disparity among the races. In the Obama era, we have witnessed massive protests in the streets and buildings set ablaze as frustrations for the absence of racial justice boiled over. In the Obama era, we witnessed the most deadly act of racial violence in generations in a massacre at a church in Charleston,

South Carolina. The Obama era witnessed the poisoning of the water supply of an impoverished American city populated mainly with African Americans.

History will undoubtedly record the years of President Barack Obama's service as racially tense and troubling years. These years have been defined largely by Black suffering and pain. As the Obama era now comes to a close, racial tensions throughout America remain high.

In fact, if the stakes were already high, they may have just become higher.

Enter Donald J. Trump, the New York-born billionaire and real estate mogul, reality television star, and now, at the time of this writing, President-Elect of the United States of America. In the wake of his election, thousands of Americans have taken to the streets in protest as President-Elect Trump has emerged from his presidential candidacy as an international symbol of hate and intolerance, one who, for many, "represents a bigoted, misogynistic worldview and an existential threat"[5] to the security of our nation. For much of President Obama's terms in office, President-Elect Trump was one of the primary voices in America questioning President Obama's legitimacy as president by claiming that President Obama was not an American citizen, but was foreign born, baseless claims President-Elect Trump later recanted near the end of his own candidacy.

More persons voted for President-Elect Trump during the Republican presidential primaries than any other Republican primary candidate in American history.[6] Although he lost the popular vote by over 2 million votes, his primary opponent, Secretary Hillary Clinton, conceded the election to him based upon the perceived results of votes to be cast for him in the Electoral College. As a voting bloc, "Despite reservations expressed by many evangelical and Republican leaders, white born-again/evangelical Christians cast their ballots for [Trump]...at an 81 percent to 16 percent margin over Hillary Clinton."[7]

Donald Trump ran for office under the campaign slogan "Make America Great Again." Throughout his candidacy, he offered a vivid and troubling platform for how, in his opinion, greatness would return to our nation. This platform included building a multi-billion dollar wall to separate Mexico from America. He repeatedly stated that he would force Mexico to pay for it. His platform included banning all refugees from war-torn Muslim countries, including women and children, from entering the United States and creating a national registry for all Muslims currently residing within the nation, including those who are life-long American citizens.

Peaceful protesters at his political rallies were physically assaulted by some of Trump's most ardent supporters. Trump's own comments justified the use of violence against political opponents. In March 2016, after John McGraw, a white man, from Linden, North Carolina, was arrested on suspicion of assault and disorderly conduct for hitting a Black protester in the face at a Trump political rally in Fayetteville, North Carolina, Trump appeared on NBC's "Meet the Press." When asked whether he would pay for McGraw's legal fees, an offer he had previously made to his supporters who committed acts of violence against protesters, Trump responded, "I've actually instructed my people to look into it, yes."[8]

And although President-Elect Trump has disavowed their support, several hate groups, inspired by Trump's often equally hate-filled words, have become his most vocal supporters. As noted by the *Los Angeles Times*, "Trump's surprise rise to become the GOP presidential nominee, built largely on a willingness to openly criticize minority groups and tap into long-simmering racial divisions, has reenergized white supremacist groups and drawn them into mainstream American politics like nothing seen in decades."[9] Just 12 days after the election, just blocks away from The White House, at a conference held in a federal building named after President Reagan, Richard B. Spencer, the head of the white nationalist group Alt-Right, stated:

> To be white is to be a striver, a crusader, an explorer and a conqueror. We build, we produce, we go upward. And we recognize the central lie of American race relations. We don't exploit other groups. We don't gain anything from their presence. They need us, and not the other way around.[10]

Spencer's racist comments were met with ecstatic cheers and Nazi salutes.

Just weeks following President-Elect Trump's election, the Southern Poverty Law Center in Montgomery, Alabama, which tracks hate groups nationwide, released a study noting 900 reports of harassment and intimidation in the first ten days following the election. The report stated, "Many harassers invoked Trump's name during assaults, making it clear that the outbreak of hate stemmed in large part from his electoral success."[11] Social media are now filled with videos of incidents from Starbucks to Delta Airlines with Trump supporters berating fellow Americans and telling them to leave their country. Video recorded at a middle school lunchroom in Royal Oak, Michigan, and at a high school volleyball tournament in Archer City near the Texas – Mexico border featured students yelling "Build that wall!" in the presence of their Latino peers. Safety concerns amid this our nation's increasingly hostile racial climate have also led to an explosion in firearms purchases as sales have quadrupled in Black and minority communities since the election. Black gun groups have also noted that attendance at their meetings has doubled.[12]

If America's first few weeks with President-Elect Trump are any sign of the years to come, there is cause for great concern.

As tragic events unfolded in recent years across our nation, I personally found myself occupying another unique time and space as a young pastor given an international platform to speak out concerning these issues. Provided the opportunity during this particularly challenging season to be a contributor to *The Huffington Post*, my observations on race and America have quite frequently been published on the front page. With my pen, or rather, with my keyboard, I have sought to speak out with the same urgency as De La Soul two decades before, proclaiming to all who would read and hear that when it comes to the racial politics of our nation, the stakes are *still* high!

Humbly, my observations found an audience. They have been read and shared by tens of thousands of people in America and abroad. These writings have been engaged in college classrooms and small groups in congregations, read on air, included in essential reading syllabi with other commentaries on social matters, and cited in sermons and academic research. Most touchingly, these writings have reached the persons most intimately impacted by many of the tragic and racially-charged events of this era: the families of the victims.

In this offering, I present a lightly edited compilation of some of my most engaged works covering this critical period of history. These works are assembled in sections related thematically to overarching concerns. The section "On Martyrs and Ancestors" speaks about the martyrs whose blood has watered our new movement for justice and on the ancestors recently departed, from whose strength we continue to glean strength. "On Battlegrounds of Justice" speaks of the new capitals in the struggle, spaces and places where the fight for racial justice prominently rages on. "On Struggle and Strongholds" addresses the ongoing presence of systemic issues of racism and situates our present struggle as part of this historical narrative. "On Hope and Determination" offers a way forward, prophetically laying claim to victory while still in the struggle.

As an introduction to the works in each section, I include a reflection on an occasion of my personal engagement with the theme as a pastor. I attest that faith without praxis is dead. Therefore, I offer ways in which I have sought to live out my faith for the cause of justice.

This remains a critical hour for our nation. It is important to note that, even at the time of this printing, several of the cases of brutality and injustice contained within these pages remain unresolved. It is my hope that you will be inspired to learn more about the historical and present-day tragedies contained herein. On matters of race and justice in America, the stakes are exceedingly high. We urgently need a new generation of prophets in this space and in this time who are unafraid to speak truth to power and to commit themselves to working toward the liberation of all God's people.

The late 20th-century urban prophet Tupac Amaru Skakur once said, "I'm not saying I'm going to rule the world or change the world, but I guarantee that I will spark the brain that will change the world." I join with Tupac in similar refrain. As you engage my voice and the voices of others in these pages, you may find your own, and then go forth to change the world. At minimum, I pray that you are compelled to make a statement for justice and to work toward the same in whatever time and space you occupy.

For the future of our nation and our world, stakes is high!

Michael W. Waters
Dallas, Texas, November, 2016

On Martyrs and Ancestors

She entered my office one Sunday afternoon after worship, an extra large manila folder tucked under her arms. The pages in the folder were as liquid brimming at the edge of its container. All that kept the pages from covering the floor was her sure, tight grasp.

I had not known of her before she called and left a message at the church earlier in the week. Presently residing in New York City, she was a long way from home in Dallas, Texas. In her voicemail, she mentioned that she had come across several of my writings, and she was compelled to come and speak to me in person.

The folder contained files concerning the death of her college-aged daughter. She died in police custody while matriculating at a Texas junior college. The authorities claimed that her daughter may have overdosed on drugs and succumbed to them while in their custody. Her mother informed me that her daughter had struggled with depression since the tragic death of her older brother several months before, yet she could not accept her daughter's death as reported.

The facts just did not add up. Her daughter's autopsy report revealed bruises and contusions on her upper and lower torso, on her face, and on many other parts of her body. The cause of these injuries had not been explained. Additionally, video footage of her daughter's final moments in custody had not been released despite multiple requests. She believed the authorities were hiding something.

She then opened her massive files to remove a single sheet of paper. It was a picture of her daughter. Looking me intently in my eyes, she asked me whether I could help her tell her daughter's story.

Two years later, she left me another message at the church. She was about to return to Texas. This time, she was not coming alone. She had organized a nationwide gathering of mothers and sisters who had lost their children and their siblings to police brutality. After a few days of organizing and demonstrating in the area, these women desired to hold a "speak out" where they could share in community their stories of sorrow and overcoming.

Unfortunately, their attempts to reach out to older, more established churches in the city had been met with resistance. She wanted to know whether our young church would open its doors to them. Without hesitation, I said, "Yes."

One Saturday evening, I stood at the main entrance of the church as the women arrived. In many of their faces I saw looking back at me the face of my own mother. They all squeezed me tightly in their embrace as only a mother can. Most uncomfortably, they called me their hero, noting ours as the only church that was willing to open its doors to them.

Honestly, I did not feel as if I had any choice in the matter. Is this not the purpose of the church, to open its doors to the afflicted, to provide them a space to find peace and comfort in the presence of God? Our opening of a door was incomparable to all they had done and experienced. If there were any heroes present, it clearly was them.

As the program began, I was asked if I intended to offer any words. I declined. My purpose that night was to listen and bear witness to what was spoken.

One by one, these courageous women stood and spoke of loved ones lost to police brutality. They spoke of delays and denials in receiving records from the authorities. They spoke of grand juries failing to indict. They spoke of final conversations held and of dreams left unfulfilled. They even spoke of loved ones calling out for them in their dreams. For these mothers, these dreams had become nightmares.

Somehow, they also spoke of the power to forgive.

Amid their gathering, one particular statement reverberated above the others, something these women wanted to make unmistakably clear. They wanted the world to know that their loved ones were much more than mere hashtags on Twitter. They were real people with real hopes and real ambitions who suffered unconscionable pain before their demise, whose absence left a gaping hole in the hearts of all who love them. And for them, their loved ones had still received no justice.

After a repast later that evening, another mother entered my office. She too held in her arms a folder overflowing with papers. She said, "I guess you can handle this. This is the most important thing that I keep in my possession."

She opened the folder to reveal pictures of a corpse. She carefully pointed to the bruises that covered the body. She pointed to a throat that had been crushed under a knee. She pointed to a botched autopsy effort and revealed that she had to order a second, independent autopsy. The only thing that brought her comfort was her belief that her son had not suffered long. She believed that God had reached down and taken her son quickly to heaven as his broken body rested upon the cold pavement.

I nodded my head and smiled. Inside, I was unconvinced. His looked like a brutal, agonizing, and lonely death. I was angry that far too many Black bodies for far too long have met this tragic and unnecessary end. Had there truly been no way to apprehend this unarmed young man of slight frame on that bridge than to crush him under the weight of many officers?

At times, the mantle of ministry mandates that you both see and hear difficult things. Prophetic ministry then requires that you speak out concerning what you have witnessed. Always, the mantle of ministry requires courage.

The young college-aged woman's name was Ahjah Dixon. She was 23 years old. She died March 4, 2010, while in police custody in Corsicana, Texas, jail. Say her name. Continue to say her name "until justice flows like waters, and righteousness like a mighty stream" (Amos 5:24, paraphrased).

Only then shall we have no need to speak such names any more.

Black Life Is Expendable

Another day, another unarmed Black man killed by police. We grieve each one's loss and pray God's strength for their families:

Eric Garner, 43, strangled to death on a Staten Island sidewalk.

John Crawford, 22, shot to death in a Beavercreek, Ohio, Walmart.

Michael Brown, 18, shot to death, reportedly with arms raised, on a Ferguson, Missouri, street.

How often must we drink from this bitter well?

The disturbing nature of the frequency of recent news reports in which unarmed Black men have been killed by law enforcement officers is only exceeded by this fact: The act itself is deeply embedded into the racial fabric of our nation. Fifty years removed from the Freedom Summer murders of James Chaney, Andrew Goodman, and Michael Schwerner — a conspiracy allegedly enacted by Neshoba County sheriff Lawrence A. Rainey — we still face the difficult reality that for generations unarmed Black men have met their demise at the hands of those sworn to serve and to protect all citizens.

On the night of June 21, 1964, a year after the brutal assassination of Medgar Evers, three courageous young men were also killed in Mississippi. The two white men—Goodman, 20, and Schwerner, 24— each died of a single gunshot wound to the heart. The lone Black man— Chaney, 21—was tortured, then tied to a tree and beaten with chains, before ultimately being shot three times. Here, even amid brutalities, a clear distinction was made concerning the value of Black life: The white lives ended immediately, with diabolic mercy, and the Black life was made to suffer greatly before finally being terminated. In the search for these three men after their disappearance, eight more Black bodies were found, discarded like rubbish across Mississippi lakes, forests, and plains. Undoubtedly, law enforcement had a hand in these deaths as well—likely Sheriff Rainey, notorious for intimidating and killing Blacks.

Mine is not an indictment of all police officers. There are many men and women who put their lives on the line for the public good each day. Some I have been blessed to call mentor or friend. Many officers themselves have lost their lives. I honor their memories and ultimate sacrifice even as I offer gratitude for those who continue to work with great integrity to keep us safe.

Yet unquestionably, there is cause for great concern, as I believe that a critical mass of law enforcement officers finds Black lives expendable. Toward this, I see this likely cause: *There is a racially motivated culture of fear that overassigns threat to Blacks, especially, but not exclusively, to Black males, even when no justifiable threat is present.* Recent findings from the American Psychological Association support this fact, stating, "Black boys as young as 10 may not be viewed in the same light of childhood innocence as their white peers, but are instead more likely to be mistaken as older, be perceived as guilty and face police violence if accused of a crime."

Historically, Black bodies have been considered expendable and easily replaceable. Tens of millions of Africans were brought to this nation as slaves because Black life was considered expendable. If an African became gravely ill or died while in forced voyage to the "New World," he or she was just thrown into the sea. While Black life was considered expendable, the supply of other Africans on the continent was considered inexhaustible. In future voyages, other Black bodies would substitute for any losses en route.

During American slavery, Black babies and children were used as bait to lure alligators from the swamps for capture. This sometimes resulted in the maiming or death of these Black children...but then Black life was considered expendable. The United States Public Health Service used Black men to test the impact of untreated syphilis from 1932-1972, resulting in the death of many Black men and in the infection of their partners because Black life was considered expendable.

Environmental racism places the urban poor near landfills and factories that cause increased rates of cancer and other diseases because Black, and more broadly poor lives, are considered expendable. Levees in New Orleans were poorly maintained and constructed near poor Black communities, resulting in massive flooding after Hurricane Katrina because Black lives are considered expendable. Blacks receive harsher penalties for the same crimes as whites, and, according to a recent Stanford University report, the disproportionate rate of Black imprisonment may actually encourage white support of racially driven tactics such as stop-and-frisk because Black lives are considered expendable.

The expendability of Black life also extends to our national foreign policy. America's response to acts of genocide, religious persecution, and the spread of infectious disease on the continent of Africa today is oft times delayed, if acted upon at all. When it comes to foreign policy, African Black lives are considered especially expendable, their difficulties rarely considered our priority.

Of course, Black life is not expendable! No life is, for all life has great value. Yet the treatment of Black life as expendable reveals our deep and abiding malfeasance. We often fail to see the face of God in the face of our neighbor, especially if that neighbor is darkly pigmented. Since all human life was created in the image of God, we are guilty of no less than the desecration of God's image when we ignore the brutalization of our neighbors, whom we are commanded to love as ourselves (Mark 12:31).

It was while traveling the road to Damascus that Saul had an encounter with the resurrected Christ, himself a victim of fatal brutalities at the hands of law enforcement. To Saul, Jesus posed this powerful inquiry; "Why do you persecute me?" (Acts 9:4).

For the recently fallen, Jesus surely weeps and asks his question anew: "Why do you persecute me?" Maybe it is because we see Christ as we increasingly see each other, and Black life—as expendable.

The Life and Death of Lennon Lacy:
Strange, Still

The animus for *Time* magazine's "song of the 20th century" was a photograph of a Southern lynching. A Southern lynching would often draw an entire region of spectators together for a day of socializing. Small children were even present in the crowd, lifted high upon shoulders for an uninterrupted view of the day's fatal proceedings. It was a strange, albeit frequent, Southern spectacle. One that claimed many Black lives.

Given the frequency of this horrid practice, and the abundance of lynching photographs in circulation, many that doubled as postcards, it is unclear why one particular photograph troubled, then inspired Abel Meeropol, a New York English teacher and poet. Yet it did. Unable to free his mind of this troubling image over several days, Meeropol sought consolation through his pen. As ink dried upon its canvas, its residuum formed words that have haunted generations, words etched into our collective memory as lyric by the incomparable Billie Holiday:

> *Southern trees bear a strange fruit,*
> *Blood on the leaves and blood at the root,*
> *Black body swinging in the Southern breeze,*
> *Strange fruit hanging from the poplar trees.*

Now 76 years after its initial recording, there is still cause to sing this sorrowful song.

On August 29, 2014, another Black body was added to the crowded annals of those swung by the Southern breeze. In a cruel twist of irony, the body of 17-year-old Lennon Lacy was found swinging not upon a Southern tree, but upon a Southern swing set—the first in a litany of strange facts surrounding his death. Authorities in Bladenboro, North Carolina, abruptly ruled Lennon's death a suicide, declaring that he was depressed, and closed the case in five days.

Still, many questions remain.

Why did authorities fail to place bags over Lennon's hands to prevent contamination and preserve DNA from a possible struggle?

Why didn't authorities take any pictures at the scene of Lennon's death?

Why were the shoes found on Lennon's feet not the same shoes that he wore when he left home?

Why were the shoes found on Lennon's feet a size and a half smaller than his foot size?

Why were those same shoes removed from the body bag between the time his corpse was placed in the body bag and the time the body arrived at the medical examiner's office?

Strange.

Very strange.

Strange, still, is an independent examiner's conclusion that Lennon's death being a suicide is virtually impossible given Lennon's height, weight, and the items found at the scene.

The circumstances surrounding Lennon's death, however, begin to lose some of their strangeness when the fact that he was in an interracial relationship with a white woman in an area still rife with racial tension, and where the Ku Klux Klan has an active presence, is brought to the fore. History has taught us time and time again that when authorities move too quickly to close a case, a cover-up is afoot. With so many questions surrounding Lennon's death, the move to close his case remains startlingly strange, and it is cause for great concern. Thankfully, the FBI is now investigating the case.

Strange, still, is how justice for so many Black lives remains so fleeting.

Strange, still, is how swiftly certain tragedies that befall Black lives are swept under the rug.

Strange, still, is the spectacle of a Southern lynching upon a swing set, a symbol of youthful euphoria now rendered the site of a Black youth's strangulation. Of Meeropol and Holiday's "Strange Fruit," the late jazz writer Leonard Feather penned that it was "the first significant protest in words and music, the first unmuted cry against racism." The very nature of a lynching is to render the victim forever mute — asphyxiating in suspended space — the violent snapping of the neck.

While Lennon Lacy is forever muted, we who love justice must become for him as Meeropol and Holiday: an unmuted cry.

We must continue to write Lennon's story.

We must continue to sing Lennon's song.

We must continue to seek answers to strange circumstances.

We must continue to seek justice for another Black life, a life, strangely, still, gone too soon.

Kendrick Johnson: Good Kid, Mad System

On January 11, 2013, Kendrick Johnson's body was found unceremoniously disposed of in a rolled-up wrestling mat at Lowndes High School in Valdosta, Georgia—as though his young, Black life did not matter. Three months earlier Compton, California's Kendrick Lamar had released his critically acclaimed, now classic debut album, *good kid, m.A.A.d. city*. In the former of two title tracks, Lamar vividly articulated his experience coming of age amid the tripartite pressures of peers, police, and an ever-present societal insanity that encompassed it all. In lyrics, Lamar offered this disturbing revelation of his perceptions of self and security: "For the record I recognize that I'm easily prey." Near the song's conclusion, Lamar poignantly inquired of us, "Can we live in a sane society?"

In truth, there is but one word that can properly summarize the insanities that have plagued the investigation of Kendrick Johnson's death, one word that fully conveys the unyielding injustices done to the 17-year-old's body and his memory: madness. The case has been similarly "mad" in its adjective state meaning "completely unrestrained by reason and judgment," "incapable of being explained or accounted for," even "disordered in mind." Johnson's body was discovered lying headfirst in the center of a 6 x 3-foot wrestling mat. An autopsy first conducted by the Georgia Bureau of Investigation concluded that Johnson died of positional asphyxia, and his death was deemed accidental by the Lowndes County Sheriff's Office. A private pathologist hired by Johnson's parents, however, arrived at a starkly different conclusion: "unexplained apparent non-accidental blunt force trauma to Johnson's neck."

Sheer madness!

Blunt force trauma was not the only disturbing discovery made by the private pathologist. Also discovered? Newspapers. Yes, newspapers that had been stuffed into Johnson's corpse. After the initial autopsy, Johnson's organs were claimed to have been naturally destroyed. The prosecutor made the determination to discard Johnson's organs before returning his body. Subsequently, the funeral home decided to fill the void left in Johnson's body with newspaper. Although the Georgia Secretary of State's official statement was that the funeral home failed to follow "best practices" with Johnson's body, and that there were other materials far more suitable for filling the body, they concluded that the funeral home did not break any rules.

Unadulterated madness!

What has yet to be discovered is over an hour of video footage from cameras trained on the gymnasium's entrance at the time of Johnson's death. Also unaccounted for are over four hours of footage on two other cameras that might reveal who else may have entered or exited the gym. Grant Fredericks, a U.S. Justice Department consultant and FBI contract instructor hired by CNN to analyze more than 290 hours of footage from 35 cameras (after CNN won a suit to obtain the videos) concluded that the footage had "been altered in a number of ways, primarily in image quality and likely in dropped information" and "information loss."

Irreconcilable madness!

There, too, is the Johnson family's legal team's conclusion that at least two of the persons responsible for Johnson's death, once school peers of Johnson, are the sons of a local FBI agent.

Reprehensible madness!

Then there's this: The official claim by authorities that Johnson met his demise attempting to retrieve an athletic shoe that had fallen into the mat. Such a pitiful insinuation of Johnson's death brings to mind the historic castigation of Black youth. The claim draws from the same poisoned well that depicted Black youth without wit in late 19th- and early 20th-century caricatures placing their heads directly into the mouths of alligators and lions.

There has been great cruelty in this madness.

All of the madness surrounding Kendrick Johnson's death has been maddening for his family, for his friends, for all who seek justice and love mercy. It is this madness, the sheer insanity of this system of injustice, which includes his peers and the police alike, that has moved Kendrick's parents to engage in civil disobedience while seeking justice for their son, actions that have caused this grieving yet committed couple to be arrested. The hallowed words of Dr. Martin Luther King, Jr. become imperative here: "An individual...who willingly accepts the penalty of imprisonment in order to arouse the conscience of the community over its injustice, is in reality expressing the highest respect for the law."

We are in this family's debt. May God strengthen them in their resolve.

Kendrick Lamar's painful testament of being easy prey amid his peers, the authorities, and an overall system of injustice proves itself a parallel narrative for Kendrick Johnson. How daunting to be the prey of such powerful predators! Yet when placed in its proper context, while maddening, the madness surrounding this case has not been surprising. For generations, Black people have often faced a dual injury that is first caused by their victimization and then advanced through fleeting justice within the justice system.

Thankfully, a new investigation has been opened into Johnson's death. Let us pray that in these new attempts to seek justice for Johnson, a mad system comes to its senses.

We must not lose any more kids.

The Sound of God's Grief in Charleston

"And do not grieve the Holy Spirit of God..." —*Ephesians 4:30*

As Christ was being baptized in the Jordan River, the heavens opened above him. John the Baptist, Christ's slightly older cousin, forerunner of the faith, testified before the gathered assembly that he saw the Holy Spirit descend on Christ as a dove.

Ever since John's testimony, the dove has been a symbol of the Spirit of God.

Present in the epistle written to the Church at Ephesus is an expression of the Spirit's capacity to grieve. It is one of the clearest characterizations of the Divine, that God intimately experiences suffering alongside God's creation. It reveals an immanent God not content in transcendently traversing human concern, but who is vulnerable enough to share in the human experience, weeping and grieving in solidarity with us.

As worshipers gathered together to study the scriptures and to offer their petitions before Almighty God at the historic Emanuel African Methodist Episcopal Church in Charleston, South Carolina, a gunman entered that sacred and sanctified space.

Inconceivably, he felled nine of the faithful present.

As a result of the horror now inflicted in Charleston, families mourn, and a church, city, and nation remain in utter shock. Prayer circles now form on sidewalks, and prayerful petitions now reveal palatable pain as tears descend like rain to the earth below.

Yet this massive grief is not restricted to our terrestrial plane. Indeed, the very Spirit of God is grieved! Dare it be asked what the sound of God's grief is like?

Is it the sound of a million weeping widows receiving their loved ones back from war?

Is it the sound of one million Mamie Tills mourning over one million Emmetts, one million Sybrina Fultons mourning over one million Trayvons and one million Samaria Rices mourning over one million Tamirs?

Is it the sound of tens of millions of Africans while crossing the Atlantic, wailing in the hulls of ships?

Is it the wailing of tens of millions of their descendants separated upon the auction block?

Or is it a pain so deep that tears fall, yet no sound is made?

This is what it sounds like when doves cry.

Pray for Charleston.

Pray for the world.

Deep in the Heart of Texas

"The stars at night are big and bright/
Deep in the heart of Texas..."

Texas is an immensely popular state. It ranks high among the states in our union with an international profile. Texas boasts three of the fastest growing regions in America along with three of the ten most populous cities. The state's low cost of living along with its thriving business community is attracting new residents seeking fresh starts and new opportunities for success.

Last week Sandra Bland made her southward odyssey to Texas to begin a new job that was awaiting her at her alma mater, one of Texas's most storied historically Black institutions of higher learning, Prairie View A&M University.

Yet Texas is also a deeply troubled state. When you look past the veneer of towering skyscrapers and rolling plains, you discover heart-wrenching realities. Texas ranks near the top among all states in overall poverty rates and at the very top for percentage of residents without health insurance. My own city of Dallas ranks number one in the country for both neighborhood economic disparity and childhood poverty. Oftentimes our state's legislature has proven to be a willing accomplice in these unspeakable crimes against the human body and soul.

Look deeper still and you will find an even greater tragedy, one that impacts, upon many planes, these unfortunate realities: Texas's terrifying legacy of racism. Just as the echoes of liberation reached the Texas coast two years delayed, today true liberation in Texas often still appears delayed, if not outright denied. Many of the most gruesome lynching events in American history occurred within Texas's borders, events so gruesome that they gained national attention: from the Dallas lynching of Allen Brooks in 1910 to the Waco lynching in 1916 of Jesse Washington, who was castrated, fingers cut off, and whose body was lowered and raised over a fire for two hours before being dragged through town and his body parts sold as souvenirs.

However, one need not look so far into Texas's history to feel racism's sting. There is the 1998 dragging death of James Byrd, Jr. in Jasper. Mr. Byrd remained conscious for the majority of the time that his body was scraped against the pavement at increasing speeds until both his head and right arm were severed. There is the 1999 Tulia drug scandal in which 40 innocent African Americans were falsely charged with drug crimes. There is the 2001 Dallas fake drug scandal in which primarily Mexican immigrants who spoke little English were arrested on drug charges, yet the planted evidence proved not to be drugs but gypsum.

Not to mention Texas's ongoing legacy of voter suppression.

And this year, thanks to the work of the State Board of Education, Texas students will officially study rewritten histories in schools because policy makers have removed the legacy of racism from the textbooks, opting to minimize the influence of slavery in our nation and in Texas by renaming the Trans-Atlantic Slave Trade the Triangular Trade Route, suggesting that human contraband was just a small trade good among many and that the American Civil War was a conflict born of state's rights and not slavery as explicitly stated in the state's historical documents.

As our nation continues to stumble along the path of racial tension and issues of police brutality, it appears as if Texas is beginning to emerge as a state particularly and uniquely hostile to Black women. Within the span of a single year, three instances of Black women being terrorized in Texas have reached the national stage.

Last August, police in Forney pulled over and held at gunpoint Kametra Barbour and her carload of four children, all under the age of 10, although neither the car nor the passengers matched the description given to police in the 911 dispatch. In June, 2015, we witnessed a 15-year-old girl, Dajerria Becton, slung to the ground, head shoved to the ground and then placed under the knee of a McKinney officer after a pool party. And now, Sandra Bland, stopped for failure to use her traffic signal and arrested in Waller County while en route to begin her new job, mysteriously found lynched a few days later.

For every native Black Texan who has ever traveled interstate roads through rural Texas and for every Black college student who travels these roads that wind through small towns and counties between school and home, it is well known that you must obey every traffic demand. Over-obey it if you can. The penalty can prove costly, yes, even deadly. In 2015, there are still some Texas towns that local Blacks advise less informed Blacks not to stop in, not even for gas.

How someone can go from driving to a new job in Texas to dead in a Texas jail in a matter of days is unfathomable to everyone except those of us who are from Texas. As Ms. Bland traveled deep into the heart of Texas, she undoubtedly encountered the racism that has long abided there.

I believe that Texas can become a great state. I believe it can become a state where all children are fed. I believe it can become a state where the sick are cared for. I believe it can become a state where laborers are paid fair wages, where "affluenza" is appropriately diagnosed as privilege, and where our diversity is embraced as our strength. However, to get there, we must finally come face to face with Texas's racist palpitations.

In Hebrew Scripture, we encounter King David, a man who abused his great authority, caused undue harm to a woman, and then sought to cover his tracks by staging her husband's death. The Prophet Nathan confronted David concerning his great sin against God. Seeking repentance for his sins, David sang in prayer to his God, "Create in me a clean heart..." (Psalm 51:10).

As we wait in pain for more information concerning Ms. Bland's death, it is well past time for our nation, and yes, the State of Texas, to repent and to pray to God for the same.

Amen.

She Held Us All: A Tribute to Amelia Boynton Robinson (1911-2015)

In the spring of 2007, while serving as the founding director of Southern Methodist University's Civil Rights Pilgrimage, a traveling study seminar to cities and sites significant to the American Civil Rights Movement, I led our group composed primarily of SMU undergraduate and graduate students into the National Voting Rights Museum in Selma, Alabama. Sitting inconspicuously in the corner near the entrance was an elderly woman with bright, beaming eyes. My dear friend and our Selma guide, Joanne Bland, excitedly said to us, "You are going to meet history today. That is Amelia Boynton Robinson!"

Many in our group stood bewildered, yet with a sense of great anticipation due to Ms. Bland's proclamation. They knew neither the woman seated, nor her contributions to history. My mouth dropped in awe, and my legs froze in place. Amelia Boynton Robinson was a long-time leader in the Selma struggle. She invited the Rev. Dr. Martin Luther King, Jr. to join the Selma struggle leading up to its climax in the spring of 1965, driving to Atlanta, Georgia, to extend the invitation in person.

Ms. Boynton Robinson and others were engaged in a decade's old organizing effort to secure the right to vote for the Black majority of Dallas County, Alabama, a place where Sheriff Jim Clark presided with cruelty, intimidation, and violence. She was essential to the planning of the Selma to Montgomery March, and she was present in Washington, D.C., when President Lyndon B. Johnson signed the Voting Rights Act of 1965. A year earlier, Ms. Boynton Robinson courageously became the first African American to run for Congress in the State of Alabama.

Our firstborn child was only six months old that blessed day in Selma. I will never forget how Ms. Boynton Robinson held him close in her arms while seated in that corner as our group continued its tour of the museum. When she learned that our travels would lead us through Tuskegee, Alabama, she invited us to her home where, a few days later, we found unspeakable treasures from the days of the American Civil Rights Movement and sat at her feet to glean from her wisdom.

When we departed from our initial meeting with Ms. Boynton Robinson that day at the museum, we immediately crossed the Edmund Pettus Bridge. With my son affixed to my chest in a *Baby Björn carrier*, I wept. I wept deeply. I wept until I could weep no more.

I cannot say exactly what caused me to weep. Maybe it was because I knew the fate that awaited my ancestors as they first crossed this bridge on foot. Maybe it was because I knew that my feet were standing upon sacred ground, ground watered by my ancestors' blood and tears. I cannot say exactly, but years later, I still feel the power of the emotion that swept over me that day upon that bridge.

Even then, I knew intimately that one day this day would come, a day when this beautiful angel and drum major for justice would depart from us. After 104 well-lived years, Amelia Boynton Robinson made her final march through the Gates of Heaven. May God give strength and comfort to all whom she loved and to all who loved her.

As my son sat next to me this past winter at a Dallas movie theater to view *Selma*, Lorraine Toussaint, who brilliantly depicted Ms. Boynton Robinson in the film, entered a scene. I turned to my son and whispered, "You met her in real life. She held you in her arms." His eyes widened as he again faced the screen. The newfound knowledge gave him a deep sense of pride, and he became fully invested in the film.

As concerns of police brutality and voter disenfranchisement continue to dominate headlines, Ms. Boynton Robinson reemerges for us as an important figure for our present struggle. In the first chapter of my book *Freestyle: Reflections on Faith, Family, Justice, and Pop Culture*, I write, "With saddening regularity, we are losing the heroes of the American civil rights movement, leaders and foot soldiers whose fearless efforts secured for us the freedoms enjoyed by millions today...The passage of time has not alleviated all destructive and oppressive forces that seek to cause harm. In reminiscing over the courage of previous generations, anchored by their faith in God and in sharing [their] stories, I pray that we too arise within this generation to meet the challenges of our day."

Indeed, may we face the concerns of our day with the same courage and fortitude that Ms. Boynton Robinson faced them in days past. Now dearly departed, she has fully invested this sacred work into our hands.

Ms. Boynton Robinson made her transition with a certain historical flare. On a day touted as Women's Equality Day, a day commemorating the 95th anniversary of the passage of the 19th amendment, she reminded us that that historic day secured the vote for white women alone, and that women of color had to continue to fight for that right for many decades. In a week where we remember both the 10th anniversary of Hurricane Katrina and the 60th anniversary of the lynching of Emmett Till, her transition reminds us of the long narrative of Black struggle upon these shores and of those whose selfless sacrifices have worked to secure for us all a better day.

In truth, as she crossed that bridge on Bloody Sunday, March 7, 1965, and as she endured state troopers beating her mercilessly and pumping her with tear gas at point blank range —the result of which almost killed her, irreparably damaging her vocal cords and dramatically deepening the tone of her voice—she held us *all* in her arms. She courageously carried us toward freedom and toward the fundamental right of all citizens of this nation: the right to vote.

She deserves no less honor than that of a founding mother of a new republic, one truer to its bold claims than the U.S. republic at its founding. As the struggle continues, we will forever hold her in our hearts.

Rest well, Amelia Boynton Robinson. See you in the morning!

Of Bees and Butterflies:
The Monumental Life of Muhammad Ali

To appreciate fully the monumental life of Muhammad Ali, consider the location of his birth. Ali was born Cassius Marcellus Clay on January 17, 1942, in Louisville, Kentucky. During America's Antebellum period, Kentucky was a Northern-border slave state.

Louisville itself was home to a major U.S. slave market. From Louisville, first upon the Ohio River, then down the Mississippi River, human captives were shipped southward to be sold or delivered to the highest bidder. After the American Civil War, Kentucky remained home to heinous acts of racial intimidation. Whippings, shootings, and lynchings accompanied the rise of numerous Ku Klux Klan chapters across the state.

Ironically, a city and state once known for the interstate trade of humanity in bonds and for denying Black people their human dignity produced the freest Black man to walk— better still, to soar — upon these shores. Ali's life proved a study in defiance to systems and structures designed to clip his wings and to cause him to remain earthbound. He freely and openly declared to the nation and to the world truths that he and his people had long been denied.

American racism is no less than a physical war on Black bodies and a psychological war on Black souls. Racism's greatest cruelty is that after several generations, it begins to destroy from within. Malcolm X, once a friend, teacher, and confidant to Ali, addressed the cruelty of self-hate during a funeral for Ronald Stokes, who was killed by the Los Angeles Police Department in 1962 at a mosque known for monitoring police activity. X inquired of the mourners:

> *Who taught you to hate the texture of your hair? Who
> taught you to hate the color of your skin...Who taught
> you to hate the shape of your nose and the shape of
> your lips? Who taught you to hate yourself from the top
> of your head to the soles of your feet? Who taught you
> to hate your own kind...You should ask yourself who
> taught you to hate being what God made you.[13]*

In thrilling, earth-shattering defiance, Ali dared to love himself, and he fearlessly boasted in his God-given truth. To systems that declared that Black people were unattractive and undesirable, Ali declared, "I'm pretty!" To systems that reduced Black masculinity to that of a child wherein grown men were called boys, Ali not only declared that he was a man, but he told the world, "I'm a 'bad' man!" To systems that sought to reduce him to a status of inferiority, Ali declared, "I'm the greatest!" And to a world cruel to Africa and to the African Diaspora, a world that sought to trample both underfoot, Ali declared, "I shook up the world!"

Ali was beautiful. Ali was strong. Ali was free. And Ali knew it from the depths of his soul.

Ali was so free and he dared to live so freely that he fearlessly defied the United States government. He surrendered his titles, and, at the time, his reputation by refusing to be drafted into what history now records as an unwise war. Ali famously stated, "I ain't got nothing against no Viet Cong; no Viet Cong never called me nigger." He was a champion of his race and of his faith, a global ambassador of goodwill.

Even as his body was ailing, Ali continued to defy systems and structures and assert his God-given truth and the beauty of his people. In the face of the Islamophobic rhetoric sweeping across America and dominating headlines during the current presidential campaign, Ali stated:

> *We as Muslims have to stand up to those who use Islam
> to advance their own personal agenda...I believe that
> our political leaders should use their position to bring
> understanding about the religion of Islam and clarify
> that these misguided murderers have perverted people's
> views on what Islam really is.[14]*

Throughout his monumental life, Ali fully embodied his chosen name, Muhammad, meaning "one worthy of praise." He was so great and beyond definition that ultimately Ali had to define himself. As he sought to give rightful testimony to his unmatched brilliance in the boxing ring, he looked not to entities formed by human hands, but upon things molded by the hand of God. As he danced gracefully around the ring, he was as one floating like a butterfly. As he unfurled punishing blows against his opponents, he was as one stinging like a bee.

Butterflies are best known for the process of metamorphosis that they endure. Once a caterpillar bound to the earth, the butterfly emerges from its chrysalis with wings and takes flight upon the air. The bee is best known as an agent of pollination. It takes flight from flower to flower, bearing upon itself a life-giving substance. It ensures that new flowers bloom, that new life breaks forth in a new generation.

Indeed, Ali was both butterfly and bee. He was a metamorphosing presence who spread love in the face of racial hatred, and who instilled love of self to a people maliciously programmed to self-hate. He was a life-giving presence who spread peace and justice everywhere he landed.

Nothing in Ali's monumental life was given to him. He earned it all. He earned his titles. He earned our respect. Now, like butterflies and bees that have soared in the heat of the day, he has earned his rest.

Rest in peace, Champ.

Alton Sterling and the Ritual Performance of Black Death

On July 5, 1852, Frederick Douglass, that great 19th-century abolitionist, orator, writer, and statesman, delivered one of his most stirring addresses at Corinthian Hall in Rochester, New York. Douglass had been invited to speak before an assembly gathered at the hall in continued celebration of July 4, America's annual ritual and performance of independence. Instead, Douglass's words were anything but celebratory as he condemned the hypocrisy of celebrating independence while an entire nation of people—his people, Black people—remained in bonds. A former slave who had escaped to freedom, these were bonds that Douglass, himself, knew all too well. Douglass spoke:

> *What, to the American slave, is your 4th of July? I answer; a day that reveals to him, more than all other days in the year, the gross injustice and cruelty to which he is the constant victim. To him, your celebration is a sham; your boasted liberty, an unholy license; your national greatness, swelling vanity; your sound of rejoicing are empty and heartless; your denunciation of tyrants' brass fronted impudence; your shout of liberty and equality, hollow mockery; your prayers and hymns, your sermons and thanksgivings, with all your religious parade and solemnity, are to him, mere bombast, fraud, deception, impiety, and hypocrisy—a thin veil to cover up crimes which would disgrace a nation of savages. There is not a nation on the earth guilty of practices more shocking and bloody than are the people of the United States, at this very hour.*

During the early hours of July 5, 163 years removed from Douglass's poignant address, just moments after another day in another year of America's annual ritual and performance of independence had concluded, Alton Sterling, 37, a father of five, was standing outside a Baton Rouge, Louisiana, convenience store selling CDs. He was soon confronted by two police officers who demanded that he get on the ground. Standing, and with his hands raised up in the air and to the side, Sterling did not immediately comply with their directive. Sterling was subsequently tackled and thrown down to the ground. The two officers ultimately pinned him down to the ground.

Sterling appeared to struggle with the officers even as his arms were pinned down to the ground under their full weight. The officers withdrew their guns. An officer exclaimed, "He has a gun!" A few swift moments passed before Sterling's body was riddled with bullets at point blank range, the bullets entering and exiting his chest. However, when later interviewed, the owner of the convenience store, who witnessed the entire confrontation, stated that only after Sterling had been fatally shot had a gun been removed from his pocket. The owner further stated that at no time did Sterling place his hand in his pocket to retrieve his firearm.

The last two years of American life in particular have been marked by a new ritual and performance: the filmed ritual and performance of Black death. These filmed deaths of Black people have become as consistent and as predictable as fireworks on the 4th of July. In viewing these deaths, the corporate refrain of "What did I just watch?" has become all too familiar.

As police officers tackled Eric Garner two Julys ago and placed him in a chokehold, and as Garner struggled for air and declared, "I can't breathe!" upon a Staten Island sidewalk, and as we, as a nation, witnessed life expire from his body, we exclaimed, "What did I just watch?" As police officers exited their cruiser and immediately shot 12-year-old Tamir Rice while he played with his toy gun in a Cleveland playground, we exclaimed, "What did I just watch?" As film was finally released of Chicagoan Laquan McDonald's death over a year after his demise, and we witnessed police officers unload 16 bullets into his teenage frame, we exclaimed, "What did I just watch?" Even as an officer removed Sandra Bland one July ago from her vehicle and mounted her on the ground for failure to use a signal when changing lanes, we exclaimed, "What did I just watch?"

Yet there is an added torture to bearing witness to these filmed atrocities. There is the grim knowledge that often the final gruesome act in America's ritual and performance of Black death is to remove all responsibility for the death from the police officers who perpetuated the violence and to lay all responsibility exclusively at the feet of the deceased. This, in fact, may be the most shocking aspect that accompanies this Black death. Rarely has any living person been found guilty; not in the death of Kendrick Johnson, not in the death of Lennon Lacy, and not in the death of Freddie Gray. The Black dead are often both victim and suspect.

Rather mysteriously, the body cameras on both officers were somehow disabled in their confrontation with Sterling. Thankfully, the confrontation was recorded by bystanders. Still, if history forecasts the future, the mere presence of film does not ensure that any indictment or penalty will actually follow. All that is guaranteed is that we now have another life to mourn and another ritual performance to view. No longer is there a veil needed to cover up crimes that would disgrace a nation of savages. We are the savage and savaged nation, and our shockingly bloody rituals and performances are available on demand.

Terence Crutcher and the
Multiform Nature of Black Pain

Speech Delivered by the author on September 22, 2016, in Dallas, Texas.

At the same time that a bullet pierced through Terence Crutcher's frame, 50,000 volts of electricity pulsated through his body. Friends, it is this startling reality surrounding Mr. Crutcher's demise that has weighed most heavily upon my consciousness. It is the multiform nature of his pain.

Just think of his threshold of pain as he was lying upon the ground unattended to, shot and tasered at the same time. I am confident that this only intensified the agony of his final moments. I pray that God might somehow bring peace and comfort to his family.

However, in many ways, Mr. Crutcher's death is analogous to the injustices that continue to befall Black America. In this nation it has never been just one thing that sought to do us harm, but many things, and at the same time. As we look across the nation, it is not just joblessness but also failing schools. It is not just poverty but also food deserts. It is not just the prison industrial complex and The New Jim Crow but also healthcare disparity. It is all these things, and much more, and it is all of them at the same time.

So yes, while it is clear that enough is enough and that we demand an immediate end to police brutality, we also demand more, for we stand against anything that stands in opposition to Black life. Yes, we demand an end to police brutality, but we also demand an end to contaminated water supplies from Flint, Michigan, to Sand Branch, Texas. Yes, we demand an immediate end to police brutality, but we also demand an immediate end to the criminalization of our children and the school to prison pipeline.

Yes, we demand an end to police brutality, but we also demand an end to the suppression of our voting rights. Yes, we demand an end to police brutality, but we also demand an end to the criminalization of Blackness, be it our natural hair or our names passed over on resumes in the workplace.

For as we gather tonight, I join with Christ in declaring that the "Spirit of the Lord is upon [us] ... to proclaim release to the captives, recovery of sight to the blind, to let the oppressed go free, to proclaim the year of the Lord's favor" (Luke 4:18–19).

And so, if our persecution be multiform, so must be our response. We must rally, and we must vote! We must pray, and we must organize to change policy! We must boycott, we must divest, and we must reinvest within our own communities! And we must continue in our demands until justice flows like waters, and righteousness like a mighty stream!

On Battlegrounds of Justice

We were the only ones present without guns. To the north of us were heavily armed Black Nationalist groups in rank and file in front of the mosque. Standing in similar formation to our south was a heavily armed anti-Muslim group.

All of us were surrounded by heavily armed law enforcement. S.W.A.T. stood ready in armored tanks. Snipers were visible on rooftops. Mounted police and police cruisers were dispersed on the side streets. A helicopter hovered above us.

There we also stood, a peculiarly fashioned group. We were a middle-age white male pastor of a historic downtown church, a young white female Muslim civil rights leader, a young Latino Muslim educator, activist, and veteran, and two Black pastors, a middle-age female pastor and me. Amid hundreds of rounds of ammunition locked and loaded in automatic weapons, we had come to provide a nonviolent witness with threats of violence unfolding before us.

We stood together, shoulder to shoulder, intermittently facing north and south, beside a boulevard named after that great 20th-century drum major for peace. Unfortunately, like many streets bearing his name across America, Martin Luther King, Jr. Boulevard in Dallas is known more as a cauldron of poverty and violence than as a haven of peace and justice. At the foremost southwestern portion of the boulevard, just before the bridge, six liquor stores rest upon two blocks beside a pawn shop. Adjacent to them are apartments that appear as if directly lifted from the scripts of *New Jack City* or *The Wire*. Here, side streets perpendicular to the boulevard serve as pathways of prostitution and sex trafficking.

Travels northeast along the boulevard reveal abandoned and dilapidated buildings, convenience stores with grossly inflated prices, and a check cashing business. While a few Black-owned businesses exist, they do so beside an infamous car wash, a hub of drug trafficking and murderous violence. Interestingly just a block away sits the headquarters of the nation's oldest Black chamber of commerce, and beside that is the Martin Luther King, Jr. Community Center, a place where Daddy King dedicated a statue in honor of his slain son 40 years ago.

Across from the King Center sits a historic high school. While visiting the school a few years ago, I was dismayed to discover a science lab classroom void of science lab equipment. Several young church members and their parents complained of substitute teachers teaching for entire semesters, the school unable to fill its open teaching positions.

Adjacent to the school sits a historic Lutheran Church, once the headquarters of Dallas's civil rights movement, its priceless stained glass windows recently vandalized. The culprit was a young man who suffers from mental health challenges who, like many in our community, often roams and sleeps on the streets. Not far from the church is our community's only major grocer, a place my wife once left in disgust after she removed a two-year-old expired jar of mayonnaise that had sat unattended for so long that dust had settled on its lid. Our community is a food desert.

The boulevard dead-ends as it enters the grounds of the largest state fair in the nation. Historically the fairground remains the site of the largest single-day induction by the Ku Klux Klan in American history. On October 24, 1923, 5,631 new members took the oath of allegiance to the KKK along with 800 women who joined the Klan auxiliary. Our city once boasted the largest KKK chapter in the nation, and many of the city fathers were active members. While the fair has earned as much as $37 million dollars in 24 days, it remains surrounded by two of the city's most impoverished zip codes.

We have marched many times upon the boulevard. We marched here for jobs and justice in a city where poverty increased by 40 percent over the first decade of the new century, a city that leads America in childhood poverty for cities over one million residents. We marched here in solidarity with Muslim Americans being terrorized across North Texas. We gathered here to hold vigil for nine persons slain at Mother Emanuel A.M.E. Church in

Charleston, South Carolina. We gathered here to rally for an end to gun violence even as murders and violent assaults increased across the city. And here we were, again, unarmed, yet surrounded by big guns, advocating for peace even as we were seeking justice.

In many ways, the boulevard is a microcosm of the struggles still faced by Black America. Along the boulevard we find evidence of wealth and health disparities, of struggling schools, of increased violence, and an entry point to mass incarceration. The boulevard is the main thoroughfare of a community in despair, a place named after a man with a great dream that is instead a reflection of his worst nightmares.

For us, this place has become a battlefield of justice.

Upon today's battlefields of justice, the issues are always multifaceted and complex. The challenges facing us are so great that they demand we take a stand, even if we must stand in a place of danger. Our faithful witness is imperative in an ever-maddening world. If we do not stand, who will?

Therefore, we boldly stood in the middle of everyone. Should anyone have fired their weapon, we would have been in the direct pathway of the gunfire. By many, we were the smallest group present. Still, it was important that we were there. Our witness was to proclaim boldly that despite the severity of the issues facing us, violence is never the answer. We stood together shoulder to shoulder on King Boulevard in the tradition of Dr. King, our witness to declare, "The old law of an eye for an eye leaves everybody blind."

As we bowed our heads to offer prayers in the traditions of our faiths, threats were hurled on either side of us. Suddenly, the northern group advanced southward. Before we knew it, our small group was on the outside looking in as all the groups with guns converged.

Thankfully, by the grace of God, there were no additional casualties that day on the boulevard. We are already stretched thin tending to the wounded daily populating the street. As each of the groups dispersed, it was painstakingly clear that our battle for justice is far from over.

Any Negro Will Do

Any person who does not understand the fury and pain present within the African American community related to injustices enacted by some police need only look to Forney, Texas, a small town located 20 miles east of Dallas.

One late August evening, Kametra Barbour, along with her two children and two godchildren — all under the age of 10 — were driving through town. Suddenly, their nightmare began.

Ms. Barbour was pulled over by Forney police officers who exited their vehicles with guns drawn. Each passenger was ordered to place their hands out of the windows. Ms. Barbour was then ordered to exit her vehicle and to walk backwards, her hands lifted above her head. As she was being handcuffed, she cried aloud, and in distress, "What is going on? Oh my God, you will terrify my kids!"

An officer responded, "We got a complaint of a vehicle matching your description and your license plate, waving a gun out the window."

Only they had not.

Several moments before, a call was placed to 911. The operator was informed that four Black men in a beige or tan-colored Toyota were speeding down the highway, the driver with a gun in his hand. Soon after, another call informed that the car was exiting the freeway. As she drove, Ms. Barbour happened upon that same exit.

Instead of stopping a vehicle matching the description from the 911 call, officers took creative license in their interpretation of the details. The beige or tan-colored Toyota creatively became a burgundy red Nissan Maxima. A male driver was creatively exchanged for a female driver. Four passengers creatively became five, and many of those passengers creatively transformed from adults into children. The small matter of the license plate number not matching became part of their creative ingenuity.

A dashboard camera in the police cruiser captured this unfortunate incident in its entirety. Had it not, it might be easily dismissed by those who refuse to recognize that such atrocities occur with regularity, negatively impacting the trust of the African American community.

Unbelievably, an even greater offense has been committed against the Barbour family. The Forney police department has rejected any admission of error in stopping Ms. Barbour, and they have not fully acknowledged the terror their actions caused this young family.

Or was it an error? Could it be that *any* Negro would do?

Could it be that, in a nation that has legalized racial profiling through such policies as "stop-and-frisk," the persecution of pigmentation makes African Americans indistinguishable from each other in the eyes of the law — so much so that *all* are feared as imminent threats? How else can one explain how officers could be *so* incredibly wrong about such a clear description? Could it be that they saw a Black driver on a dark highway, and that was enough?

Three years ago, while I was driving under the speed limit in Dallas with my uncle, one of my best friends from college, and my then four-year-old son, officers pulled up alongside me, then quickly, behind me, with lights flashing. I pulled over. As police approached on both sides, flashlights beamed into our vehicle. When an officer approached my window, he asked me a peculiar question: "What do you do?" The inquiry caught me off guard. I responded, "I'm a pastor."

Suddenly, it all became clear. I was driving my wife's vehicle. A practicing attorney, my wife still had a law school decal on the back of her vehicle. The officers saw three Black men in a vehicle bearing a law school decal and *knew* that the car must have been stolen. Each adult male in that vehicle that evening had earned a graduate degree or had completed graduate hours. One was in the process of completing a dissertation. However, no level of success or achievement has ever insulated the African American community from such disturbing encounters. Not that success or achievement should matter, as all people deserve to be treated with dignity and with equality under the law.

Unfortunately, on any given day, any Negro will do!

Our saving grace that evening was that two attorneys, my wife and another college friend, were trailing us. I shudder to think of what could have happened to us had those women not been present. I shudder to think what could have happened if the car Forney police pulled over had been occupied by one Black man, or three Black men, or even five Black men as passengers. What could have been their fate?

It is a historic and tragic remembrance that many innocent Black men and boys were lynched by mobs after an accusation of rape made by a white woman. Whether or not the rape actually occurred was inconsequential. Lynch mobs were known to apprehend, brutalize, and then hang the very first Black man that they encountered. *Any* Negro blood would satisfy their bloodthirstiness. In some cases, the lynch mob would grow to become a rioting mob leaving dozens of Blacks killed and whole neighborhoods destroyed.

During the Forney stop, Ms. Barbour's young son exited the vehicle with his hands raised above his head and inquired, "Are we going to jail?" I weep knowing that even as a young African American child, with hands raised, that child could have been fatally engaged by police as a threat.

Four decades ago, the late, great Marvin Gaye inquired through lyric, as Ms. Barbour did that August night, "What's going on?"

The answer that we have awaited for so many years may have long been under our noses. When it comes to explaining certain brutalities, *any* Negro will do.

Mortal Men and the City of Baltimore

"When sh*t hit the fan, is you still a fan?" — Kendrick Lamar

On the most talked about track ("Mortal Man") on the most talked about album (*To Pimp a Butterfly*) of the year, Kendrick Lamar engages in a fictional interview with the late Tupac Shakur. Near interview's end, Lamar inquires of Shakur, "I can truly tell you that there's nothing but turmoil going on, so I wanted to ask you what you think is the future for me and my generation today?" In words recorded two decades before, Shakur states, "I think that n***** is tired of grabbing sh*t out the stores and next time it's a riot there's gonna be...bloodshed for real. I don't think America know that...It's gonna be like Nat Turner, 1831."

As violent protests now rage in the City of Baltimore in response to the horrific death of 25-year-old Freddie Gray, a Black man whose spine was severed 80 percent at his neck while in the custody of Baltimore police, Shakur's words prove prophetic. In the wake of a multitude of horrific Black deaths at the hands of police officers across the country, there is a sense of a generation that has grown weary of these atrocities, and, as such, has also grown weary of the suggestion of peaceful protest as a means of bringing these brutalities to an end.

Interestingly enough, Shakur's prophetic words find their historical complement in the words of Dr. Martin Luther King, Jr. In March 1968, a month prior to his assassination, Dr. King boldly stated, "It is not enough for me to stand before you tonight and condemn riots. It would be morally irresponsible for me to do that without, at the same time, condemning the contingent, intolerable conditions that exist in our society. These conditions are the things that cause individuals to feel that they have no other alternative than to engage in violent rebellions to get attention. And I must say tonight that a riot is the language of the unheard."[15]

It would be the grossest of errors to look upon the uprisings in Baltimore solely in the context of Baltimore. What has occurred there is but the next chapter in a centuries-old American narrative in which unarmed Black women and men are killed in the custody of police officers. Yet while this narrative is generations old, the advent of new technologies and social media platforms has not only magnified the pains suffered, it has ensured that evidence of the same go farther, wider, and faster than ever before.

Multitudes have protested peacefully in Baltimore and around the nation. Yet a question now arises as to what should be done in response to the violent protests presently unfolding on the streets. Both King and Shakur, themselves young Black men who were victims of horrific acts of violence, would caution America to respond responsibly. For only to address the violence of a minority of protesters and not the systemic violence that has set the stage for their responses would be to reveal historical ineptness.

Recently, I was invited to make a presentation at a national conference for large churches in a major U.S. denomination. In my presentation, I provided instructions for how churches could involve their members in social action initiatives. About halfway through the presentation, a woman was clearly perturbed by my verbal challenge for all churches to do more to fight for justice in the communities that surround them than to engage exclusively in mission trips abroad. In her frustration, she stated, "I would rather help people who are not responsible for their suffering than those who are."

This woman's misguided statement revealed the faulty lens through which many persons look at Baltimore, Ferguson, Staten Island, and far too many other communities to name. These persons, rather than hearing the voices of a people long suffering under intolerable conditions, conditions that have claimed the lives of Freddie Gray, and countless others, have exclusively attributed the causation of the people's pain to the people themselves. Hence, the blood on the hands of a nation is washed away.

Mortals are defined by limitations. What happened in Baltimore is but a sign of a people who can take no more. While we may not agree with the response, we cannot overlook the cause of the response. Just as Lamar listened to frustrations rendered a generation ago, it is time for us all to listen anew.

At the conclusion of "Mortal Man," Lamar poses one final question to Shakur. Speaking in metaphor concerning the butterfly and the caterpillar, Lamar notes, "Wings begin to emerge, breaking the cycle of feeling stagnant. Finally free, the butterfly sheds light on situations that the caterpillar never considered, ending the internal struggle." To all of this, Lamar asks, "What's your perspective on that?" The song concludes as Lamar seeks an answer, yet Shakur offers no response.

It is suggested that at song's conclusion, Lamar provided an insight absent in Shakur's initial articulations: a way to change the world without also destroying the world in the process. Indeed, the violent protests in Baltimore should end, for the violence will not bring about the ends needed within the community. As King also stated, "Violence as a way of achieving racial justice is both impractical and immoral... because it is a descending spiral ending in destruction for all. The old law of an eye for an eye leaves everybody blind."[16] However, our nation must actively listen to what these actions are saying to us. Then, and only then, will we be able to shift the conversation and offer opportunities to secure the changes we seek and so desperately need.

I am not a fan of violence, but I am a fan of the people being heard. Now that it has hit the fan, I pray that we open our ears to hear the cries of a people far too long trampled upon, a people who can take no more. I also pray that we are able to change our world without destroying our world in the process.

Swimming Pools

"Pour up (drank), head shot (drank), sit down (drank), stand up (drank), pass out (drank), wake up (drank), faded (drank), faded (drank)." — Kendrick Lamar

The 20th-century struggle for racial justice, equal access, and equal protection under the law known as the American Civil Rights Movement unfolded over many decades and upon multiple planes. Most commonly, however, when the masses reflect upon these struggles, the planes of struggle considered are public schools, lunch counters, and buses. Yet one of the most significant planes upon which this critical history unfolded were places of recreation: beaches and swimming pools.

From the Atlantic waters of Myrtle Beach to the Pacific waters of Santa Monica, to public pools in municipalities throughout our nation, the opposition to the integration of these public places was fierce. In some cases lives were lost, even if an integrative act was unintentional. A 1919 race riot in Chicago resulted from the stoning and subsequent drowning of African American teenager Eugene Williams, who violated the unwritten segregation of Lake Michigan after he mistakenly swam into "white-only" waters.

Among the primary historical motivations for standing in defense of beaches and pools against integration was that these settings were perceived as highly sexualized environments. It was believed that white women in bathing suits would be harmed if allowed to interact with the hypersexualized Black male. Therefore, the virtue of white women, as well as concern for the perceived uncleanliness of Black bodies, which purportedly would bring disease to the water, was enough to support and encourage strong, even violent opposition to the desegregation of beaches and pools.

Now, in the 21st century, as disturbing video of African American teenagers in McKinney, Texas, many donning bathing suits, continues to spread rapidly throughout all media, swimming pools once again emerge as a place of struggle. First verbally, then physically attacked by adult civilians, these teenagers, many of whom reside in the community, were made to sit on the ground by police. Some of these teenagers were even handcuffed while their white counterparts meandered about without any police interference.

As an officer slammed a teenage African American female to the ground, drew his gun on those concerned for her well-being, then placed the full weight of his body upon the young woman's back, history repeated itself.

Dr. Martin Luther King, Jr. once recounted one of his most difficult experiences as a father: the day that he had to tell his children why they would not be afforded entry into a popular, yet segregated amusement park.[17] It is always difficult when young people are terrorized, unfairly excluded from the joys of life. Unfortunately, time and time again, we have borne witness to this exclusion. The impetus for this is one of the greatest threats before us as a nation — civilians and law enforcement officers drunk on their own errant perceptions of racial superiority and power.

One of the first lessons given a beginning swimmer is not to drink the water. Drinking pool water will make you sick. The same is true for those who continue to drink from the long polluted pools of racism and xenophobia. Without question, the videos of the incident in McKinney show that those who have drunk their fill of the pool are now inebriated with the fear of others, and stumble and fumble through life, placing our safety and security at risk.

Interestingly, bodies of water, both natural and human made, have set the stage for divinely inspired acts of liberation. From the waters parted at the Red Sea that set a nation free to a providential encounter with Christ at the pool of Bethesda that healed a man of a lengthy illness, water holds great significance to our freedom narrative. May then the McKinney pool serve as the water of baptism for a new generation of activists committed to the liberation struggle.

It is still far too early to tell what will ultimately emerge from all of this. Painfully, this generation knows all too well that just because an incident is captured on camera does not mean that justice will be served. While awaiting the findings, not only of the McKinney investigation, but of countless police-involved incidents across the country, it is clear that American justice needs to be checked into rehab.

Prayerfully, then we can once and for all drain this polluted pool.

It's Complicated:
On Tubman, Race, and Progress in America

After many years of struggle to achieve equal opportunity and accommodations for African Americans in this nation, Dr. Martin Luther King, Jr. is famously quoted as saying, "What good is having the right to sit at a lunch counter if you can't afford to buy a hamburger?" Dr. King's statement powerfully and succinctly illuminates the complicated nature of race and progress in America. Quite often progress is followed by the immediate recognition that much more progress is needed to achieve equality among the races in America.

Hence the complicated nature of reactions to U.S. Treasury Secretary Jacob Lew's announcement that 19th-century abolitionist Harriet Tubman will replace President Andrew Jackson on the face of the American $20 bill. In so doing, Tubman will become the first African American featured on American paper currency and the first woman featured on American currency in more than 100 years. This is undeniably a historic achievement.

On one hand, if there is any historic American personality deserving of this honor, it is Harriet Tubman. She was a model American at a time when many states regarded her as property instead of as a citizen. After escaping to freedom in the North, she courageously returned to the South hundreds of times to lead others born into slavery into freedom via The Underground Railroad. Tubman embodies all that should be celebrated and honored in America: bravery, ingenuity, intelligence, loyalty, and strength.

Furthermore, a retrospective view of President Andrew Jackson proves him unworthy of the honor that had been bestowed upon him by placing him on our currency. The legacy of America's seventh President is, at best, problematic. During his lifetime,

Jackson personally held hundreds of human beings in captivity and forced them to work as free labor. He built his wealth on the weary backs of the captives, who harvested cotton on his over 1,050-acre plantation. A runaway notice from Jackson himself offered a $50 reward for the return of "a Mulatto Man Slave." Repugnantly, the notice also offered the captors "ten dollars extra for every hundred lashes...to the amount of three hundred."[18]

Jackson's cruelty reflects the worst of our nation and is without honor. If anyone deserves to be removed from America currency, it is Jackson. Unfortunately, Jackson will not journey far. His image will still be captured on the back of the $20 bill.

On the other hand, it proves exceedingly difficult to be completely celebratory of this swapping of images given the gross racial wealth disparity still present in our nation. According to the U.S. Census Bureau, 27.4 percent of Black people live in poverty, the highest percentage among all racial and ethnic groups in America.[19] In 2014, among Black people who were unemployed, 23.7 percent had attended college, 15.4 percent had bachelor's degrees, and 4.5 percent had advanced degrees.[20] Disturbingly, by percentage points alone, there are more unemployed Blacks with advanced degrees than there are unemployed Asians overall. In America, a Black college graduate has the same job prospects as a white high school dropout or a white person with a prison record.[21] And while the median wealth of white families increased from $138,600 to $141,900 between 2010 and 2013, the median wealth of Black families decreased from $16,600 in 2010 to $11,000 in 2013.[22] When it comes to Black economic progress in America, our nation is headed in the wrong direction.

The economic disparity among the races in this nation is not accidental, but intentional, and multifaceted. It reeks of the smoke that bellowed from the ruins of Tulsa's Black Wall Street and is stained red by the innocent blood that flowed down the street of the same. It looks like the redlining of communities and the construction of urban highways that destabilized the economies of the urban core in the mid-20th century. It sounds like names believed to be too ethnic that appear atop the resumes of qualified applicants who do not get called in for an interview.

It is J. Edgar Hoover's COINTELPRO. It is President Richard Nixon's War on Drugs. It is President Ronald Reagan's "Reaganomics." It is President William Jefferson Clinton's Crime Bill. It is the suffocating reality and presence of American racism and its economic manifestations. Just as King openly questioned the value of having access to a lunch counter but lacking the financial resources to order from the menu, there is a certain unintended cruelty in placing our nation's greatest Black abolitionist on currency at a time when many of her descendants are struggling to make ends meet.

Still, like many, when Tubman's $20 bills are released, I will be in line at the bank with unyielding excitement. I will proudly display them and distribute them to my children. Yet as I pass public inner city schools that are still without adequate resources to properly teach our youth, as I pass the unemployment line, and as I witness another family in line at the grocery store wrestling with hard decisions in the checkout line, seeking to determine what items they must leave at the store because they cannot afford it all, I will question whether or not this is the freedom for which Harriet Tubman fought.

Then, if I have it on me, I will hand them a Tubman $20 to assist with the grocery bill.

American Justice in
Black and White (and Green)

This week, in a Tarrant County, Texas, courtroom, Ethan Couch was handed a two-year prison sentence as a condition for his continued probation stemming from an intoxicated manslaughter conviction. In 2013, Couch killed four people when he rammed his truck into them while driving under the influence of alcohol. Two other persons were seriously injured, thrown from the bed of Couch's truck during the crash.

Prosecutors argued that Couch, then 16, deserved a 20-year prison sentence for his crime. The defense countered by arguing that Couch suffered from a condition called affluenza, which is defined as "the unhealthy and unwelcomed psychological and social effects of affluence regarded especially as a widespread societal problem such as feelings of guilt, lack of motivation, and social isolation experienced by wealthy people." They argued that his parents' wealth veiled him from understanding the consequences of certain actions. Consequently, he should not be unduly punished for said actions.

The court sided with the defense. Couch was given a 10-year probation and ordered to abstain from alcohol consumption. He was also ordered to complete rehab and reportedly did so at a luxury rehabilitation facility that included horseback riding among its featured activities.

In December, a video surfaced of Couch violating the terms of his probation. He went missing after failing to show for a subsequent meeting with his probation officer. Now fugitive from the law, Couch was found several weeks later at a Mexican resort town near the Pacific Ocean. While in Mexico, he reportedly consumed large amounts of alcohol and consorted with prostitutes. He was extradited back to the United States to await sentencing.

Last April, Allen Bullock participated in protests in Baltimore, Maryland, following the death of Freddie Gray, the 25-year-old Black man who died of spinal cord injuries while in police custody. On April 25, 2015, Bullock climbed atop a police cruiser and damaged the vehicle by breaking its windows with a traffic cone. Mr. Bullock, who had minor offenses as a juvenile, was arrested, and his bail was set at $500,000. He spent 10 days in jail as his parents struggled to make bail for their son. (Comparatively, the bail set for two of the police officers arrested for homicide in the death of Freddie Gray was $250,000 and $350,000, respectively.)

On March 29, Bullock was sentenced to serve 12 years in prison. Ultimately, all but six months of his sentence was suspended. Bullock must serve five years of probation, complete 400 hours of community service, get his GED, and write a letter of apology to the Baltimore City Police Department.

These cases are a prime example of American justice in Black, white, and green. Both cases involve 19-year-olds. One is white. One is Black. One comes from wealth. One comes from one of the most impoverished communities in America. And far too often in this nation, the right combination of race and resources results in leniency from the justice system, and the wrong combination results in undue punishment.

Couch's actions killed four and seriously injured two. Bullock's actions hurt a car. Couch became an international fugitive from justice. Bullock voluntarily turned himself in to authorities.

For his crimes, Couch's parents offered to pay for his stay at a $450,000-a-year luxury rehabilitation community. For his crimes, Bullock's bail was set at an amount well beyond his parents' means.

And although Bullock will serve approximately one-fourth of Couch's sentence, the court actually sentenced him to eight years longer than a court sentenced Couch. Given the gross wealth disparity among Blacks and whites in America, in which the median wealth of white households is 13 times the median wealth of Black households, these injustices in Black, white, and green may only increase, unless new approaches are pursued.

Thankfully, also this week, the U.S. Department of Justice's Bureau of Justice Assistance, in partnership with the Center for Court Innovation, announced that the Dallas County Public Defender's Office was one of 10 applicants nationwide to receive a 2016 Community Court Grant Program award. The Dallas City Attorney's Office in partnership with the Public Defender's Office is establishing Dallas County's first-ever county/municipal partnership to set up Dallas County's first-ever felony community court. The South Dallas Second Chance Community Improvement Program Court (S.C.C.I.P.) will receive a $200,000 grant to fund a two-year program targeting young adults in South Dallas.

Dallas is the epicenter of poverty in America. It leads the nation in childhood poverty for cities over one million residents. Here, poverty increased by 40 percent between 2000–2012. Recently, two South Dallas neighborhoods made the FBI's notorious list of the 25 most violent communities in America. Dallas was the only Texas city to make this list.

The newly funded community court, which will operate in South Dallas, will "respond to quality-of-life crimes by ordering offenders to pay back the communities they've harmed through visible community service projects such as painting out graffiti, beautifying neighborhood parks and cleaning up litter and debris from public streets."

The community court will also "link offenders to drug and alcohol treatment, mental health services, job training, and public benefits; services designed to help them address the underlying issues fueling their criminal behavior."

After successfully completing the program, defendants will have the opportunity to have their records expunged. National research has proven the community court a model to effectively reduce crime, to reduce substance use, and to increase services to victims, all the while saving taxpayers money and improving the public's confidence in the justice system.

If affluenza works as a defense, it would seem logical that poverty would too. It has not. Therefore, courts like S.C.C.I.P. are a welcome and necessary approach for restorative justice, especially for historically marginalized communities that have for far too long suffered greater penalties then their wealthier, and often whiter, counterparts when appearing before the judicial system. Still, more must be done to ensure that all persons—regardless of their financial means or their racial heritage—receive equity before the courts.

Instead of paying for a luxury rehabilitation center, maybe Ethan Couch should have gone through S.C.C.I.P. Thankfully, many who would not be granted nor could afford such luxuries as Couch will have this opportunity. And we will all be the better for it!

On Struggle and Strongholds

I took a seat next to my friend, the imam, near the front of the mosque. A camera was trained on us as the Friday worshipers filled the space, some sitting on chairs, and some sitting on the floor below. The camera ensured that we would engage an even larger audience than the one gathered before us. Our dialogue would be streamed across the globe.

I first met this young, charismatic, highly intelligent imam in June of the past year. We gathered together to hold vigil for nine precious souls martyred two evenings before at Mother Emanuel A.M.E. Church in Charleston, South Carolina. The weight of this massacre weighed heavily upon our shoulders.

Two months after our vigil, I visited Mother Emanuel. I was in Charleston to speak on a conference panel. While there, I requested to stop by the church so that I could pay my respects.

Outside, the church was adorned with flowers and stuffed animals. A large wall that had been erected was completely covered with condolences. Sunlight reflected brightly upon the white edifice, betraying the brutalities that had unfolded there.

I entered the lower level of the church, where Bible study was traditionally held. There, I looked upon the bullet holes that had pierced the walls. A man named Brother Nathaniel, a trustee at the church, became my guide. He pointed over to the circular tables erected near the side of the room. "That's where most of the killing took place," he said. He mentioned there were more bullet holes in the floor beneath the tables. I could not bring myself to look.

I did look upon the door to the Pastor's Study. It was behind that door that the late state senator and pastor's wife and one of his daughters took refuge. That door served as the only barrier between them and the horrors that unfolded on the other side.

Before departing, I left a copy of a tribute that I had written the night of the tragedy. The church secretary graciously received the tribute and stated that it would be shared with the congregation.

The space reminded me of another church that I had visited several times before while leading civil rights pilgrimages across the Deep South. Like the lower level of Mother Emanuel, the lower level of the 16th Street Baptist Church in Birmingham, Alabama, was the site of unspeakable horrors. Neither space is particularly extraordinary, save for the tragic events that unfolded there, which bespeaks the fact that these tragedies could have taken place anywhere.

Just as I had looked upon the space where a domestic terrorist with a bomb took the lives of four little girls on September 15, 1963, I was now looking upon the space where a young domestic terrorist armed with a handgun—yet driven by the same hate—took nine lives over half a century later. The tragedy in Charleston bore witness to the fact that the same struggle for racial equality and the same stronghold of racism was still before us, only separated by time and space.

It was for this reason that I had been invited to the mosque. My friend, the imam, was concerned for the Muslim community. Daily, words of hate and acts of hate were being levied against them. Presidential candidates were calling for Muslim Americans to wear identification eerily similar to Hitler's orders that Jews do the same in Germany. Other candidates were calling for special patrols in Muslim neighborhoods. Both were calls motivated by misappropriated fear.

Times were particularly challenging for Muslims in our North Texas community. Armed protests were being held outside their mosques. The Ku Klux Klan threatened to hold its own protest of a local mosque as well. Men in fatigues and masks carrying AR-15s followed closely behind female worshipers wearing hijabs as they made their way to their mosques. An anti-Muslim organization went so far as to publish the home addresses of prominent Muslim leaders on a website, an intimidation tactic directly from the days of the civil rights movement when addresses of activists were published in the local newspapers.

A young Muslim boy who proudly brought his homemade clock to school to show his teachers was arrested and accused of making a bomb. This incident in a Dallas suburb made international headlines. A Muslim man new to the country was gunned down outside his apartment while watching snow fall for the first time. A Muslim mechanic was shot and killed as his assailant hurled Islamic slurs. One night, while gathering together for a rally against gun violence, we received news that the windows in the home of a Muslim family had been broken with large rocks.

Humbly, the imam had previously quoted my words during his sermons delivered at the mosque, but I was physically present that night to offer words of encouragement myself. My words were intended to strengthen this community by reflecting upon the historic and present suffering of my own people and of how we have worked together to overcome. I offered that there were no monolithic approaches in the Black community to overcoming oppression, but I did offer one approach that has been most meaningful to me: the way of faith.

As I spoke, I shared that our community's faith had strengthened us for generations, enabling us to keep moving forward in the face of unspeakable horrors and of great odds placed against us. I shared that their community's faith would also see them through. Tens of thousands streamed our conversation and offered kind words for our time of sharing. The worshipers present were especially kind and gracious.

Yet I was drawn to the young children who were present and who later came to shake my hands and to extend their gratitude. Watching these Muslim children and my own children, who had accompanied me that night along with my wife, playing together later as the adults congregated in extended conversation, illuminated the importance of our present work in the world. Our work is necessary so that our youth will not face the same struggles and strongholds of generations past. This must be our singular mission and our greatest goal.

Stakes Is High:
Redeeming the Soul of America

On June 18, 1996, a famed hip hop trio that hails from Long Island, New York, released its fourth studio album. Trugoy, Posdnuos, and Maseo, better known as De La Soul, entitled the album *Stakes Is High*. On the title track, Posdnuos and Trugoy bemoaned societal ills with clever puns and powerful insights;

> *"Gun control means using both hands in my land."*
> *"Investing in fantasies and not God, welcome to reality,*
> *   sometimes it's hard."*
> *"Neighborhoods are now hoods 'cause nobody's neighbors."*

Eighteen years later, these lyrics still speak to issues confronting our nation.

In light of an alarming succession of grand juries that have failed to render an indictment against police officers using deadly force against unarmed Black men, including Staten Island native Eric Garner, another one of the song's lyrics demands our consideration:

> *"A meteor has more rights than my people."*

Despite compelling video evidence of Garner's murder, a grand jury decided not to indict the officer responsible for his death. Undoubtedly, for Garner's family, and for all who love justice, it would appear as if extraterrestrial properties do indeed have more rights than Black men.

If nothing else, such properties may have more protection.

Unlike Garner, who repeatedly cried "I can't breathe!" as his life slipped away upon the pavement, meteorites are cherished as precious gems, housed safely within the corridors of museums or securely in private collections to protect them from undue harm. For generations, there has been great tension between the Black community and police, largely due to the undue harm the Black community has suffered at their hands. Riots in Watts in 1965 and in South Central in 1992 were fueled by injustices enacted by police, as well as within the justice system. Buildings in Ferguson were recently ablaze after a grand jury found no probable cause to indict Michael Brown's killer.

Our country is now at a critical juncture as the public's confidence in the police and in our justice system has waned, especially since both are deemed credible threats to the public's safety. Like previous generations, this present generation has already known too many unnecessary tragedies. It is a generation overrun with martyrs, and, with the advent of social media, their accompanying hashtags:

> #TrayvonMartin
> #HoodiesUp
> #JordanDavis
> #MusicUp
> #EricGarner
> #ICantBreathe
> #MichaelBrown
> #HandsUpDontShoot
> #KendrickJohnson
> #RenitaMcBride
> #JohnCrawford
> #TamirRice
> #EzzellFord

Who will be next?

Violence is far too often not just a subtext, but the main text in American society. We remain the most violent industrialized nation in the world. No place in our society has remained untouched. Not suburbia. Not the halls of higher education. Not grocery stores. Not even houses of worship. However, American violence proves all the more weighty when it is unjustly enacted by those who carry a firearm and a badge, and their wrongful actions appear insulated from due process by prosecutors and grand juries.

In a statement made to the White House Tribal Nations Conference in Washington, D.C, President Barack Obama expressed that all Americans should have equal protection under the law. He also acknowledged that for far too long, and in far too many communities, this has not been their experience. Obama stated, "When anybody in this country is not being treated equally under the law, that's a problem... It is an American problem."[23]

Indeed, this is an American problem, and it is a problem that has grown long in the tooth. It is a problem that challenges the very essence of all that America espouses itself to be. It is a problem that challenges America's standing and authority in the global community. How can America continue to call other nations to task for human rights violations when America cannot protect large segments of its own citizens from the same? How can America police the world when it cannot effectively police its own police? How can America effectively promote democracy when it appears that the same has not been fully granted to all its citizens?

Ultimately, our nation is not facing a law enforcement problem or justice problem. Our nation's greatest problem proves to be a moral one. At the very heart of this problem is the failure to value and respect all human life as sacred. Each life, no matter how it is pigmented or financially endowed, must be fully embraced as one created in the very image of God.

It would be unimaginable for a person who views all human life as sacred and as created in the image of God to look upon the frame of a teenager and see, not a human being, but a demon. No individual who views human life as sacred and as created in the image of God would remain unmoved by a dying person as he cries aloud for breath to breathe. And no person who views human life as sacred and as created in the image of God would kill a young child on sight.

The stakes *is* high!

The time is *now* to demilitarize the police. The time is *now* for greater community reviews of the police. The time is *now* to address the senseless loss of life that has come at the hands of far too many sworn under oath to protect and to serve. We must stand together and work tirelessly to redeem the soul of America from these brutalities.

The stakes *is* high, for when it comes to equal protection under the law, it is all or nothing.

American Terrorist

"Now if a Muslim woman strapped with a bomb on a bus with the seconds running gives you the jitters, just imagine an American-based Christian organization planning to poison water supplies to bring the second coming quicker."
—Lupe Fiasco, "American Terrorist," 2006.

One of the great honors of my life was a chance meeting with a diminutive woman named Vera Harris in Montgomery, Alabama, the widow of Dr. Richard Harris, who was a leading Black businessman and pharmacist in Montgomery. We met over a decade ago while I was a seminarian visiting the city. During the days of the Montgomery Bus Boycotts, Dr. Harris's downtown pharmacy and lunch counter provided sanctuary to Black passengers as they awaited pick up via a taxi system established by the Montgomery Improvement Association. In his book *Stride Toward Freedom*, Dr. Martin Luther King, Jr. recalled Dr. Harris simultaneously filling prescriptions and calling in rides for his patrons.

The Harris family lives in a large, beautiful home just a few doors down from the old Dexter Avenue Baptist Church parsonage. On the evening of January 30, 1956, Mrs. Harris was at home when she heard a loud explosion. She immediately knew what had taken place, and she raced from her home to the Dexter parsonage as a first responder to the act of terrorism that had just unfolded there. The parsonage had been bombed while Coretta Scott King, newborn daughter Yolanda, and a Dexter church member were inside. Dr. King, who was speaking at the weekly mass meeting, raced home as soon as he received the troubling news.

During our encounter, Mrs. Harris vividly recalled the days of the Montgomery Movement and the tensions and hostilities that filled the air. Yet there was one remembrance that emerged for me as the most gripping. When I inquired about the first bombing of King's home, she stated matter-of-factly that the sound of bombs exploding across the city was a nightly occurrence. Many nights, Mrs. Harris laid her children down to the sickening sound of bombs detonating, not somewhere in the Middle East, but in America.

In recent days, a national debate has been waged as to whether or not Syrian refugees should be granted entry into the United States of America. Opponents, including the governors of several states, argue that members of ISIS posing as refugees could enter the nation and unleash the same terror recently released in Paris. God bless the dead.

Yet in the wake of five protestors being shot while peacefully protesting the death of Jamar Clark near the Fourth Precinct police station in Minneapolis, it is once again revealed that the most longstanding and deadly terrorist groups in America have always operated under the banner of white supremacy. White supremacists have long terrorized our nation, especially the Black community, and, as such, white supremacists continue to pose the greatest threat to our national security.

The Mayor of Dallas (at whose nomination I serve as chair of the Martin Luther King, Jr. Community Center of Dallas), the Honorable Michael S. Rawlings, made national headlines this week concerning the Syrian refugee crisis. Mayor Rawlings stated, "I am more fearful of large gatherings of white men that come into schools, theaters and shoot people up." As it relates to the legacy of terror in our nation, yes, even up to the present day, this remains a legitimate concern. From the Oklahoma City bombing 20 years ago to the Columbine High School massacre in 1999, to Charleston, South Carolina, and many others places in between, white supremacy can be credited with inspiring more acts of terror upon American soil than any other philosophy.

It is well past time to shift our nation's narrative concerning domestic acts of terrorism. For centuries, for whole communities of Americans, it is not unknown threats from without, but known threats from within that have remained the greatest concern. This is not to suggest that international terrorism is not real, or that there have been no legitimate threats to our nation. America owes a great debt of gratitude to the men and women who work tirelessly to intercept and eliminate proposed acts of terror upon our nation's soil.

Still, in the total conversation of and mobilization against terroristic threats to our national security, it is imperative that the problem of American terrorists be fully included in the discussion. If we do not properly acknowledge the presence of American terrorists, and the severity of their histories of violence, we will be grossly unprepared to protect our citizens from their heinous acts of terror in the present and in the future. If our political focus remains solely on international terrorists seeking to gain a foothold within our nation, we will continue to overlook the social climate that continues to produce terrorists on domestic soil.

In no way are ISIS members heroes to be celebrated. Much innocent blood is on their hands, and, for the sake of our international community, they must be brought to justice. May God bless the dead.

Still, to date, no ISIS member or Syrian refugee has ever bombed or planned to bomb a Black church or home. Nor have they walked into a Bible study in the basement of a Black church and unleashed a hail of bullets. Neither are they at fault for the continuing epidemic of unarmed Black men, women, boys, and girls murdered by police officers in the streets of America. They have not turned our communities into militarized zones, nor have Black people mysteriously died in their prisons. God bless the dead.

In our seeking forth for justice, let us not overlook the terror long lurking inside our own doors. For whole communities of Americans, the greatest terrorist threat is not now trying to enter our country.

It has been here for a long time.

The Empire Strikes Back
(or Fear of a Black Planet)

"Excuse us for the news/ I question those accused/
Why is this fear of black from white influence who you
choose?"
— Public Enemy, "Fear of a Black Planet," 1990.

As a child, my all-time favorite movie was *Return of the Jedi*. I still remember the *Star Wars*-themed curtains that I proudly hung in my bedroom and my battery-powered light saber that glowed green in the dark. As a teenager, I was still enamored with the film, so much so that one Christmas I received a VHS box set of the original trilogy as a gift.

That Christmas, I immediately began my own *Star Wars* marathon. Despite my love for *Return of the Jedi*, I had never watched the first two films. I thoroughly enjoyed the first movie, but I found the second movie, *The Empire Strikes Back*, a discomfiting film. It did not leave me with the same triumphant feeling as the first, where Luke Skywalker destroys the Death Star, nor of *Return of the Jedi*, which ends in Rebel victory.

In *The Empire Strikes Back*, Luke endures both psychological and physiological harm. Darth Vader is revealed as his father, and his father cuts off his hand in battle. The film clearly depicts the vicious nature of empire.

Whenever empire responds to radical change, the response is always brutal. As our nation continues to bear witness to gross atrocities committed against Black bodies and Black minds, it is clear that our nation is witnessing the brutalities that accompany the striking back of an empire.

Historically, empire defines nations that hold extensive territory throughout the world, territories often claimed by brutal force.

As it relates to our nation, empire must be lifted beyond the mere notion of sovereign and expanding borders, but instead be understood as a system that controls psychologies and influences people's actions. In his book *Christ and Empire*, Dr. Joerg Rieger defines empire as "the massive concentrations of power that permeate all aspects of life and that cannot be controlled by any one actor alone...Empire seeks to extend its control as far as possible; not only geographically, politically, and economically, but also intellectually, emotionally, psychologically, spiritually, culturally, and religiously."[24]

Considering our nation's history of brutality, the most impactful and destructive system known upon these shores has been the empire of white supremacy. Disturbingly, in the face of progress, there are signs that the empire is striking back.

Whether it be the vitriol of presidential candidates with their calls to take our nation back, or a Black motorist gunned down on the highway by a plainclothes officer who did not bother to identify himself, or a young girl hurled across the classroom in her desk, it all speaks to empire as white supremacy striking back to reclaim the territory it believes it has lost. Every time another racist-themed fraternity party is planned, or we witness another miscarriage of justice against Black life in the courts, these are signs of empire striking back.

The nature of empire as white supremacy is such that fictional worlds have not been spared from its wrath. Some fans of *Star Wars* began an unconscionable protest against the forthcoming *Star Wars* film *The Force Awakens* because it features a Black man—John Boyega— as the lead actor. This is unconscionable in that Black men such as James Earl Jones and Billy Dee Williams held roles in the original *Star Wars* releases. However, when empire strikes back, it strikes back at everything, real or fictitious!

Such nonsensical conclusions birthing brutal actions are the fruits of empire as white supremacy. This empire has robbed continents of its humanity, forced conversion, and raped and pillaged in the name of God. This empire has used Black bodies as lab rats for medical research, military and civilian alike. This empire refuses to maintain levee walls but runs to build border walls.

Empire strikes with impunity.

Empire as white supremacy sees progress as decline and diversity as weakness. Therefore, empire projects fear for who we are becoming as a nation, which is a more diverse nation, and it promotes a return to segregation as the solution. At its root, empire is fear, the fear of a Black planet in which Blacks, and other historically oppressed and marginalized communities, are given seats at the table of power, a planet where all are equal and all are treated equally.

Dr. Martin Luther King, Jr. devoted two entire chapters to empire as it strikes back in his first book, *Stride toward Freedom: The Montgomery Story*. In his chapter "Methods of the Opposition," King writes in vivid detail about the various struggles that the people of Montgomery faced from the empire as they sought to gain equality under the law. This opposition included everything from espionage to "a series of arrests for minor and often imaginary traffic violations."

Again, for empire, fact and fiction are perceived the same.

The chapter is followed by "The Violence of Desperate Men." In this chapter, King recalls the bombing of his home and the bombing of other homes during the boycott. With the fear of change, empire can strike with deadly force.

Today, what continues to draw me to *Return of the Jedi* is its message of hope. This hope is the hope of a people — a diverse people — standing shoulder to shoulder to fight back against all threats of an empire. As we continue to see evidence of an empire striking back, let us awaken the force within and embrace our collective power to work together for progress and to bring about the changes so desperately needed in our society.

Even when facing empire, the force has always been strong with people committed to working together for justice.

Know Your Place, Boy!
(I Mean, President Obama)

To the present members of our United States Congress, does President Barack Hussein Obama seem to not know his place?

The latest in an overflowing, voluminous list of offences that President Obama, the 44th President in the 240-year history of the United States of America, has had to endure is that Senate Republicans have formally announced via a Judiciary Committee letter that they will not hold any hearings on any U.S. Supreme Court nominee presented by this sitting President. Senate Republicans once again appear determined to throw a wrench into the wheels of our democracy by having a seat upon the nation's highest Court remain open for an indefinite period of time, a seat vacated with the recent passing of the Court's longest-serving justice, Justice Antonin Scalia. It would be a gross misinterpretation of purpose to consider this opposition merely as political jockeying in a presidential election year. Instead, what President Obama is enduring is the same that has been endured by African Americans since the advent of this nation.

It often appears as if the majority white and male Congress is saying to President Obama with their actions, "Know your place!"

Unquestionably, President Obama fits the description of an uppity Negro. He actually thinks that being elected by the American electorate to the presidency twice with an overwhelming majority of the popular vote gives him the right to function with the full powers of that office. Misguidedly, he thinks that he can simply nominate someone and have the Senate to meet with the nominee, as has transpired with sitting presidents before him, even presidents like him who were completing the final year of their term. This former professor of constitutional law actually thinks that the rights granted to the Office of the President by the Constitution apply to him.

This boy, I mean, President, should know his place. Since he has clearly forgotten, let us benevolently offer him this quick reminder:

Never, ever look a white person directly in his or her eyes. You are not their equal. In fact, science suggests that you are not fully human. Your total value derives from being the property of your master.

If you serve your master well, you will make it to Black heaven—not to be confused with White heaven. To ensure that you understand this, when you die, we will bury you in the Black cemetery. So you will have company with Black corpses until White Jesus comes to take you to Black heaven.

Understand? Good.

Never, ever share the sidewalk with a white woman. If you see a white woman approaching, stop immediately, and cross over to the other side of the street. If you cannot make it to the other side of the street, then run. Run as fast as you can in the opposite direction. Do not fail to heed these instructions, lest we be forced to string you up on the nearest tree.

Furthermore, your entrance is always in the back, and your seats are always in the balcony. You cannot attend this school, live in this neighborhood, or eat at this counter. You cannot use this restroom or drink from this fountain. Never forget that the key to your survival is to know your place, for stepping out of place can have fatal consequences.

Obama, please do not allow your Ivy League education, your Hawaiian upbringing, or your white parentage cause you for a moment to think that you are like us. Please, open your eyes and open your ears. We have been warning you about staying in your place throughout your terms in office.

When we, the political gatekeepers of white supremacy, yelled, "You lie!" during your State of the Union address, we were really saying, "Stay in your place."

When we degradingly referred to you as a Muslim and questioned your citizenship, we were really saying, "Stay in your place."

When we waved our finger in your face upon an Arizonian tarmac, or when we refused to show up all together to welcome a sitting president into our state, we were really saying, "Stay in your place."

When we called your wife a monkey and when we called your daughter's hair un-American, again, we were really saying, "Stay in your place."

Mr. President, it is imperative that you know your place. If you don't know your place, others may be tempted to step out of place as well. It is bad enough that an entire generation of young people can see themselves in you, in the tight curl of your hair and in the hue of your skin.

To keep Negroes in their place we once made lynching a grand event. We invited the whole community to attend and to participate in these horrors, and we encouraged them to take fragments of clothing and even body parts of the deceased as souvenirs. We posed for pictures beside dangling corpses and charred bodies, and then we dragged the corpse through the streets of the Black community. In some cases, we forced Black families from their homes to view the corpse as it was being dragged down their street.

Times have changed, somewhat, and we cannot take out our aggression always in the same manner of our forbears. Still, we have our ways of keeping uppity Negroes like you in their place. So no, we will not meet with any person that you nominate for the Supreme Court.

Hopefully, this time you will learn your lesson.

Stay in your place.

Nigger.*
I mean, Mr. President.

---

* This is an extremely painful word, one levied with particular impunity against my ancestors. I do not use it here carelessly. For the reader and author alike, the word disturbs the spirit. This is, in fact, why I deploy its use here. We ought to be disturbed—deeply disturbed—at the treatment of President Barack Obama and of many Black Americans. This word, historically labeling and illuminating the president's treatment, serves as a witness to how much work still remains to achieve racial equality in America. May we all be disturbed to move into action.

Make America Great, Again?

During a recent online conversation with my beautiful, brilliant and graceful mother, she reflected upon the America in which she grew up. Born in the mid-1950s, she came of age in the 1960s in rural Central Texas. Both of her parents were educators with a combined 77 years of teaching experience.

Her parents demanded excellence from her and her younger brother, both inside and outside the classroom. They told their children that in order to compete in the world, they would have to be twice as good as white people in everything they did. In those days, America was quite degrading to my mother, to her family, and to countless Blacks across the nation. She recounted some of the degradation in vivid detail:

She recalled the "White Only" drinking fountains in public spaces.

She recalled the old, rickety, structurally unsound staircase off to the side of the main entrance that she and her friends had to climb in order to find a seat in the "Colored" balcony at the movies.

She recalled that the textbooks her parents had to drive over two hours to pick up from the now infamous School Book Depository in Dallas each year were never up to date.

She recalled that the chairs in the "Colored" doctor's office waiting room were old and wooden, but that the chairs in the "White" doctor's office waiting room were plush and upholstered.

She recalled that the streets north of the main road — which divided the town in half — where the white people lived were paved streets. Yet the streets south of the main road, where the Black people lived, were dirt roads made muddy and, in sections, unnavigable when it rained.

Even after integration, degrading words and actions were almost constantly aimed at her, her family, and many Blacks in her community.

My mother recalled that after integration, her white teacher openly spoke to her father and new colleague, marveling at how suddenly smart the "Nigra" children had become after only six weeks of learning beside the white children.

She recalled how baffled her English teacher was at her extensive vocabulary. The previous spring, my mother had delivered a speech while campaigning for yearbook editor. That fall, when my mother was a student in the teacher's class, the teacher expressed with awe that my mother used the same vocabulary in her daily conversation as she had in her speech. Her teacher was finally convinced that no one had written the speech for my mother.

She even recalled the unfortunate treatment her father received after integration. My grandfather also came of age in Central Texas at a time when the Ku Klux Klan was hyperactive. Still, he became a learned man with earned degrees in biology and education. He integrated the graduate program in geology at Iowa State University, and he presented his research on monogenetic trematodes before the Texas Academy of Sciences. Still, his white colleagues shunned him.

Adding further insult to injury, my mother recalled the time my grandfather set the plans to have a new home built for his family. He had the money for both the land and the down payment on the home. Yet when it was time to discuss the model of home he had selected for his family, his choice was denied by the contractor. A white family had also selected that model, and it had been determined that it would not be proper for a Black family and a white family to reside in the same model of home.

My mother recalled the looks of utter shock she received while working the cash register as a teenager at the local five and dime. Previously, Blacks were relegated to stocking and bagging items. She overheard a customer, gesturing toward her, say to another, "Yeah, they's even on T.V. now."

As an undergraduate student at a state university, when she received the highest score of all students in all of her professor's sections, the professor constantly brought up her grade before the class. This recognition made her feel very uncomfortable, especially since she was one of only 300 Blacks on a campus of

20,000, and quite often she was the only Black person in her classroom. When my mother inquired as to why the professor continued to bring up her grade before the class, the professor responded, "Your fellow students have been taught that they are smarter than you because you are Black." Rather than being used to make the case for equality among intellects, her achievement was used to motivate students who were told they would never be outperformed by a Black person.

My mother recalled that when she entered the professional workforce as a recent divorcée with a graduate degree in hand and having recently purchased a new home, a co-worker offered to her this failed compliment: "You are not like I was told Black people are. You don't have a bunch of babies by a lot of different men. You're educated, and you don't smell."

Then my mother told me, "I am not excited by the rhetoric of making America great again."

"Neither am I, mom. Neither am I."

Stay woke!

Trump: When Race Is as God

Eight years ago, while President Barack Hussein Obama was but a first-term senator from Illinois seeking the Democratic nomination, I was presented with a series of strange emails. The emails were an alarming mix of pseudo-biblical prophesies of imminent doom to the United States of America, her allies, and to the entire global community should Mr. Obama become the leader of the free world. Several of these emails went so far as to name Mr. Obama as the Antichrist, the eschatological biblical personality who would woo the masses and then usher the world into unprecedented pestilence and destruction.

In this current presidential election season, to the amazement of many, Donald J. Trump appears well on his way to securing the Republican nomination. Throughout his campaign, if he could offend someone, he has. He has appeared to mock the other-abled, labeled Mexicans as rapists, and proposed a ban on Muslims entering the country. Trump has even suggested a national registry of all Muslims eerily similar to the registration of Jews in Hitler's Germany.

Still, his political momentum has not waned. In fact, it appears to increase with each insult leveled at another group or personality. Most recently, he has invoked as a national threat the possibility of riots should he not receive the Republican nomination.

What could possibly be the appeal of a presidential candidate who is an unrepentant demagogue, racist, and islamophobe? How is it that Trump has so easily discarded Republican opponents with legitimate records of public service when he possesses none? I believe the answer is found entangled in the emailed propaganda I read eight years ago.

For every Antichrist, there must be a Christ. After the Antichrist comes a Messiah to redeem the land and to save the people from the wrath. In the peculiar space that is the fringes of Christian fanaticism and pseudo-biblical prophecy, Trump is as God.

Whiteness and deity have long been married in the West. From Michelangelo's 1512 fresco of a white and white-bearded God on the ceiling of the Sistine Chapel to American artist Warner Sallman's 1941 *Head of Christ,* a deity possessing European features has been the most prevailing image of the Christian God for over 500 years. In an interview concerning his 2012 book with Paul Harvey, *The Color of Christ: The Son of God and the Saga of Race in America,* Edward J. Blum offered that the image of a white Christ *trumped* Scripture for the Ku Klux Klan and was readily employed to justify their racial violence. Blum stated, "The belief, the value, that Jesus is white provides them an image in place of text."

If Obama is conceived as the Antichrist by those gathering in rallying mass in support of Trump's presidential bid, Trump is much more than a presidential candidate. In Trump, they see a national savior, a kinsman redeemer, one who now comes to reclaim and to restore America to its supposed former glory. Trump is a white Christ formed in the image of white supremacy, a prophet of American exceptionalism.

And as if in an evangelistic revival, Trump comes preaching the white gospel of supremacy. His singular sermonic topic is "Make America Great Again." This is a coded message for taking control of an increasingly diversifying nation and returning it to a time when, in Trump's own words, "You know what they used to do [to protestors] like that when they got out of line? They'd be carried out on a stretcher, folks."

As such, Dr. Ben Carson, Senator Rafael Edward "Ted" Cruz, and Senator Mario Antonio Rubio never stood a chance at securing the Republican nomination. Although they are Republicans, they are wholly other: an African American and two Latinos. While they too can, and have, preached the gospel of white supremacy, they can never be the white Christ.

In this peculiar presidential election season, race is as God. Trump is without any meaningful text. He has not presented any substantial policy or platforms. Honestly, he does not need to. People are not voting for Trump as much as they are voting for the image he reflects.

A multitude of political commentators did not initially take Trump's campaign seriously. They believed that Trump would find little appeal among the American electorate. However, the writing for a successful campaign had long been written on the wall. It began long before a self-avowed Christian and Ivy-league graduate of interracial parentage was castigated by birthers and islamophobes—Trump among them—as a Kenyan-born Muslim. It began when this Black man, our President, was called the Antichrist, the very personification of evil in the world.

This Holy Week began with Palm Sunday, which commemorates Jesus Christ's triumphant entry into the city of Jerusalem. It remains to be seen whether Trump will have his own triumphant entry come this November. For some, the political stage has been set for a white Messiah.

And Trump fits the bill.

On Hope and Determination

The once empty ballroom began to fill with bodies as hip hop soundscapes saturated the atmosphere. Young adults from across North America, in all ways diverse, from equally diverse Christian faith traditions, entered in. Standing along the periphery of the room were chaplains, pastors, scholars, and staff, equally diverse, each of whom had assembled to support these young adults in their process of spiritual discernment.

Thirteen years prior, I was one of them: a young adult in the process of discerning my spiritual calling. I too had been fortunate enough to be surrounded by a similarly vast group of diverse young adults hailing from across the nation, supported in our process by faith practitioners both gifted and committed in their mentorship of us. St. Paul, Minnesota, was our scenic backdrop for this critical engagement.

A month before that, I had finished college. Two months later, I would begin seminary. At that exact time, I was suspended in time and space between the life that I had known and a new world of experience that was fearful and foreign, yet exciting. It was good to be in the company of other young adults who were also standing in this uncomfortable tension surrounded and supported by those who had journeyed in that space before us and not only survived, but thrived.

For 13 years, my experience with the Forum for Theological Exploration (the Fund for Theological Education when I first entered) had been formational to my Christian development. From my earliest experience as a Ministry Fellow, which provided resources to create a ministry project to engage and empower adolescent young men in my community, to a scholarship to attend a conference for ethnic minorities considering the pursuit of Ph.D.s and Th.D.s, to the opportunity to serve as a mentor pastor to seminary fellows, to the opportunity to present my doctoral research before national conferences, FTE had been a central part of each season of my ministry development since college. Now, here I stood again in the strong embrace of FTE.

However, this time I stood confidently in a place in which I had not stood before. This time, I stood as the founding pastor of a growing congregation. This time, I stood as a recognized leader in my community. This time, I stood as an adjunct professor in a doctoral program. This time, I stood as an award-winning author and frequent commentator on matters of public concern. And I stood ready to pour out all that had been poured into me over many years into a rising generation of faith leaders and scholars now being nurtured under the careful support and encouragement of FTE.

After leading an idea lab at this Christian Leadership Forum, I was poised to lead the entire conference in Graffiti Worship. Graffiti Worship is a liturgical experience that I had developed and honed over several years of experimentation. Humbly, FTE had previously provided me with space to conduct this experiment.

Those who had attended my idea lab joined with me in providing leadership to our liturgical experience. Each of them sat before the congregation facing them in chairs. On either side of them butcher paper covered a long wall in the ballroom. I was also accompanied by our church's DJ, who spins records and scratches during our worship experiences at my church. I have been honored to travel with him across the country as we have led workshops and worship experiences engaging hip hop culture.

As groups of two, my fellow hip hop liturgists read lyrics from the late Tupac Amaru Shakur as if reading passages of Scripture. As they read, the DJ spun tracks from Kendrick Lamar's *To Pimp a Butterfly*, an album that offered the world a new chant for a new movement for justice: "We gon' be alright!" As they were inspired by the lyrics of Tupac—lyrics that illuminated much of the pain in the world—and as they were led by the Holy Spirit, these young faith leaders approached the wall and commenced to draw, write, and color how Tupac's words made them feel, as well as their hopes for the future for our world.

I stood in silent awe as the once blank canvas in the once empty room began to fill not just with colors and shapes, but with hope. There was the bold, illuminated red cross that stood in defiance to the evil of the world. There was the written memorial to Mike Brown, Tamir Rice, Eric Garner, and Walter Scott that declared to the world that these martyrs' names would forever be remembered.

There were the declarations that "Christ liberates!" and that "We are peacemakers!" Also present were verses of Scripture that declared both God's justice and God's hope for a better day. "Struck down but not destroyed" found its space next to "And they will beat their swords into plowshares" on the graffiti wall.

Next, wall and space were transformed into a place of intercession. Prayers were offered while facing the wall as if it were the Western Wall in the City of Jerusalem. Then commenced the laying of hands and the blessing of the liturgists who had sat before us, even as they began laying hands upon each other, blessing one another in the name of the Lord. Some lay prostrate on the floor, seemingly immersing themselves as the Spirit moved to the rhythm of the bass and the snare.

When our worship concluded, the room was slow to clear. Tears were wiped from eyes and mutual embraces were shared. I was personally blessed by words of thanksgiving for the experience that we had shared.

After several moments had passed, a once empty room was empty again. I stood there alone, gazing upon the only visible representation of the power that had been present here: a wall covered in hope. It was not a hope that avoided the truth of the challenges of our day. Nor was it a hope ignorant of the pain and suffering that fills our world. Instead, it was a powerful hope, a hope that listened to the pain, sat with the pain, cried because of the pain, and yet with determination, looked forward with hope to a newer and brighter day. It was a hope committed to working toward that end.

Our work completed, I then departed the room with hope and determination to join the others in making the world God's canvas for peace and justice.

Michael Brown and
Our Great Opportunity

The days succeeding the tragic police shooting death of an unarmed Black teenager in Ferguson, Missouri, have further affirmed or exposed several unfortunate realities present within our society today.

We live in a news media culture often shallow in depth and largely out of touch with reality — so much so that some media fail to grasp it even as it unfolds around them. From suggestions that "water cannons" be turned on peaceful protestors in Ferguson to Captain Ron Johnson being depicted as a gang member due to his Kappa Alpha Psi fraternity salutation, these unfortunate flubs have come quickly and with rapidity.

We live in a society that readily offers convenient narratives to justify violence against Black people. In the wake of his death, Michael Brown, like so many other Black victims, was depicted as a lawless drug addict who posed a clear and present danger to society. In support of this narrative, not only was a video of an alleged convenience store theft of cigars (quite unrelated to Michael Brown's death) released by the police, but also an officer took to social media to post a picture of another Black man holding a gun in his hand and money in his mouth. He then falsely claimed that person to be Michael Brown.

This further exposed yet another unfortunate reality: To some people, Blacks are indistinguishable from each other. Thus, any picture of any Black person engaged in any questionable activity will suffice for degrading the whole community.

We also live in a nation that too readily dismisses the issue of police killing unarmed Black citizens, or of any plight uniquely experienced by Black people, by pointing out that Black people kill each other daily. The issues of police brutality against Blacks and of Blacks killing other Blacks are not mutually exclusive. That is to say, one issue does not negate the other; both pose a significant threat to the well-being of society.

Furthermore, reports of police entering into a church to stymie protest efforts further suggest that very little, whether life or space, is considered sacred anymore.

Yet despite these unfortunate realities, many positive outcomes have followed in the wake of this senseless tragedy. For the last several days, social media has become a more thoughtful and justice-centered space. Reality show disputes and celebrity gossip have been replaced by posts, images, videos, and trending topics lifting up the importance of this hour.

Instead of being a corridor of narcissism, incessantly decorated with selfies, social media has served as a powerful platform to form and to reinforce community and movement.

Another generation appears to have been awakened to the power of its voice lifted in protest, and it is making its voice known. This collective voice has been so powerful that it has gained international attention and support. Thankfully, even some artists and celebrities have begun to recognize the importance of this hour and are using their celebrity to raise awareness.

Emboldened by the Ferguson movement, local movements are sprouting up across the country to push their police force toward needed reforms. Important conversations are being held concerning police wearing cameras and the community having greater review of local forces. Out of such great pain and darkness, a light has begun to appear, and with its appearance comes a great opportunity toward becoming the elusive beloved community. Here are some ways that we can continue to journey forward:

No one who has posted, shared, or tweeted an image of Michael Brown's lifeless body should ever again post, share, or tweet a *WorldstarHipHop* fight video, or any video depicting or glorifying violence. It is hypocritical to seek justice for victims of violent crimes, even at the hands of the police, and to promote and celebrate violent crimes committed within our neighborhoods and between our neighbors.

No one who cares about the death of Michael Brown, or about the violence enacted against peaceful protestors in Ferguson, can then not care about the acts of domestic violence happening between your next-door neighbors, or about the child abuse occurring on the next street over, or about the sexual trafficking happening down the block. Violence is violence, and it is meaningless to oppose violence abroad yet disregard it, in its many forms, at home.

No one who cares about the death of Michael Brown, or the scourge of police brutality, can ever choose again not to vote. Period. Not only did people die so that you could vote, people die because you do not vote. This is especially true when it comes to selecting your local leadership. If you choose not to vote, you are a co-conspirator in the problem.

In light of this great opportunity birthed out of great tragedy, we must be wary of those on any side advocating for increased arms and promoting violence, or the threat thereof, as a viable solution to our nation's problems. While the sides may appear to stand in opposition to each other, they are in fact unified in a commitment, not to self-preservation, but to mutual annihilation. The wisdom of our forebears guides us in this sacred hour with a clear and certain voice: "The old law of an eye for an eye leaves everybody blind... It seeks to annihilate rather than convert."[25]

I pray that our relevant, sustained, and commendable outrage and peaceful protest over the death of Michael Brown does not end with Michael Brown. May it enlarge itself to include a relevant, sustained, and commendable outrage against all acts of violence and injustice.

And may we not rest until justice "flows like a mighty river, and righteousness like a mighty stream."

Rebirth of a Nation

In the third chapter of the ancient Gospel narrative titled John, a religious leader named Nicodemus approached Jesus under the cover of night. Jesus stated, "I tell you the truth, unless you are born again, you cannot see the Kingdom of God." Nicodemus then inquired of The Christ, "What do you mean? How can an old man go back into his mother's womb and be born again?"

As with Nicodemus, the idea of rebirth has been a point of contention, controversy, and curiosity, a point vigorously debated among the early church councils, a point of departure among diverse adherents to the faith. Just what does it mean to be "born again"? Of many perceptions of meaning, one prominent belief is that to be "born again" is to be released from the fatal consequences of sin, which first originated with Adam and Eve and became a heritage for the entire human family, and to have the hope of a Utopian existence with God in a future time.

If America has a sin of origins, a sin deeply rooted within the nation's epistemology, it is undoubtedly racism. Permeating the soil and soul of our country even before the nation's founding, and fully grafted into our nation's DNA through its founding documents, racism is a sin long befalling America.

If the wages of sin are indeed death, America's bloody history reveals that we have been fully compensated.

In 1915, American racism may have reached its zenith with the cinematic release of *The Birth of a Nation*. Widely regarded as a cinematic masterpiece and historically footnoted as the first motion picture screened at The White House, *The Birth of a Nation's* racist depictions of African Americans — especially African American men as inherently ignorant, violent, and hypersexualized savages — aided the Ku Klux Klan, who used the film as a recruitment tool, in dramatically increasing its membership rolls. The movie reflected and exasperated fears of an American society under Black rule, fears emergent during the Reconstruction Era after Blacks were freed from slavery, en masse.

Our nation's xenophobic proclivities have caused great harm to many and have led to generations of marginalization and oppression. *The Birth of a Nation* offered a vivid portrait of White America's worst nightmare: a society run amuck by freed Blacks. The film reached its horrifying height when a white woman fled through the woods to escape a large Black male seeking to rape her.

Ironically, although commonplace, the Black male rapist was depicted by a white male actor. When finally cornered by her would-be assailant, the white woman leapt from a cliff to her death. As she fell, she incited the murderous intentions of thousands, and hundreds of real Black men became their victims. Since its release nearly 100 years ago, we have lived in an era defined by the film's cultural constructions, the greatest legacy of which is the terrifying Black man — ignorant, deviant, bent on destruction. This construction is so ingrained within our nation's consciousness that, for many, the Black man is the personification of evil.

Even as The White House is presently occupied by a biracial, African American self-identifying man and his Black family, constructions of African Americans as ignorant, violent and sexual deviants remain prevalent throughout culture and media. These constructions are not without consequence, and it has often proven fatal. In fact, it is this cruel criminalization of color that has resulted in the death of countless unarmed Blacks at the hands of police officers for generations.

As innocent blood flows in our nation's streets, parks, stoops, and stairwells, it calls for justice. As a constricted airway whispers screams of agony, it calls forth for a new day. As the body count attributed to these painful atrocities continues to rise, our nation has reached a boiling point and the calls for justice amid gross injustices has resulted in an uprising. It is in the midst of these uprisings, the likes of which we have not seen upon these shores in two generations, that America is being reborn.

Surely some are as Nicodemus, unsure, even doubtful of the possibilities of this rebirth. Jesus answered Nicodemus's concern thus: "The wind blows wherever it wants. Just as you can hear the wind but can't tell where it comes from or where it is going, so you can't explain how people are [born again]."

It may be hard to explain rebirth, but it is easy to hear.

I recently had the opportunity to address a "This Stops Today Rally" in downtown Dallas. As I panned the diverse crowd, the cries of "Black lives matter," "Hands up, don't shoot," "No justice, no peace," "I can't breathe," and "This stops today" filled the nighttime air. Under the cover of night, the mystery of rebirth once again unfolded.

I told the story of Allen Brooks, a 50-year-old Black man who had been accused of assaulting a white child. I acknowledged that any Black man accused of anything in 1910 was deemed guilty by mere accusation. When Brooks appeared in court, a mob broke into the courtroom, placed a noose around his neck, and threw him out the second floor window. He landed head first upon the ground below.

Some have stated the fall may have killed him, but he was still stripped of his clothes, then dragged by the rope around his neck to the corner of Elm and Akard Streets where he was lynched. His body would later have to be rushed out of the city as, after it was cut down, the rabid crowd still desired to burn it. When the judge called a grand jury to identify Brooks's killers, although a multiplicity of police officers was present, and although there were horrific pictures of the day's tragedy, the police officers said that they could not identity one offender.

For Allen Brooks, there was no justice.

As we gathered that night, only 0.3 miles from where Brooks was lynched, it was impressed upon me that the same sin that killed Allen Brooks in 1910, and the same sin that informed *The Birth of a Nation* in 1915, continues to claim new victims today. So as we rallied and marched, it was not just for Michael Brown, Eric Garner, John Crawford, Tamir Rice, and Ezell Ford, but for all whose names history no longer remembers but who suffered similar fates.

As we continue to lie down, march, chant, and organize for justice together, we serve as the midwives to our nation's rebirth. Our collective cries echoing forth in these winds of change signify that our nation's water has finally broken in order that justice might "flow like rivers, and righteousness like a mighty stream." America is contracting, and ours will not be a still birth. No, these present labor pains will bring forth justice and equality to all!

On account of America's many sins, we are now being redeemed *by* the people and *for* the people. Our fight is still young, and it is not without opposition. Indeed, there appear to be days of struggle ahead. Although the road ahead remains challenged, the imperative before us is clear:

Push!

Our labor shall not be in vain.

We Gon' Be Alright

Dedicated to my friend and colleague,
the Rev. Sharon Risher,
daughter of Emanuel 9 Martyr Ethel Lance

Though a terrorist enters and fells our families and pastors at
church...
We gon' be alright.
Though Congress delays our confirmation without justifica-
tion...
We gon' be alright.
Though our beauty is rejected as we dominate on courts of
grass and clay...
We gon' be alright.
Though our spines are broken in Baltimore...
We gon' be alright.
Though knees are upon our neck in McKinney ...
We gon' be alright.
Though we are thrown from desk and tumble...
We gon' be alright.
Though we are stopped and detained in Waller...
We gon' be alright.
Though we are concerned students in Missouri...
We gon' be alright.

Though we receive 16 shots in Chicago...
We gon' be alright.
Though we are five shot in Minneapolis...
We gon' be alright.
Though questions of our intellect resound from
the highest court...
We gon' be alright.
Though we see police cover-ups and falsified reports...
We gon' be alright.
Though gunmen parade in front of our mosques...
We gon' be alright.
Though denied entry at the border like Mary and Joseph at
the inn...
We gon' be alright.
Though our chained ancestors be taught as
migrant workers...
We gon' be alright.
Through many dangers, toils, and snares...
We have already come.
We gon' be alright.
Until Black lives matter...
We gon' be alright.
Until justice flows like waters...
We gon' be alright.
Let it resound loud as the rolling sea...
We gon' be alright.
As long as God got us...
We gon' be...
Alright!

It All Falls Down

"Said it's the misery of inequity/ Said it's the history of inequity/ When it all, it all falls down..."
— Lauryn Hill, "The Mystery of Inequity," 2002

More than a century ago, W.E.B. Du Bois, the first African American to earn a Ph.D. from Harvard University and one of the cofounders of the National Association for the Advancement of Colored People, published his seminal text, *The Souls of Black Folk.* Du Bois powerfully propounded in that text that the "problem of the Twentieth Century is the problem of the color-line." Truthfully, Du Bois's words not only defined America's existence up to 1903, but they readily define America's existence ever since. Ours continues to be a problem of the color-line, a problem that appears in many manifestations.

America is a nation constructed upon the shifting and unstable fault lines of racism. Racism has permeated every aspect of our nation's existence in every era of its existence. It has been an unrelenting and unyielding stain, an oozing and infected sore upon our legislatures and our economy, upon our judiciary and our public policies, upon our educational systems, and yes, even upon our religious assemblies.

Therefore, much of our nation's history can be defined by social movements to emancipate our land from the chains emergent at its founding. Ours has been a long, ongoing struggle to extend the inalienable rights once narrowly defined as the inheritance of male European American property owners to all persons resident upon these shores, both native and foreign born.

That a nation built upon racism was given a faulty foundation was not without warning. Early voices cried aloud that by constitutionalizing racism our nation was on shaky ground. From William Lloyd Garrison and Harriet Beecher Stowe to Frederick

Douglass and Sojourner Truth, from Martin Luther King, Jr. and Fannie Lou Hamer to The Dream Defenders and Black Lives Matter, and to countless others in each generation, there have been prophets to our nation who have called our nation to account for its sins against God and humanity. As a nation, we have paid a great price for not heeding their warnings.

Now new voices have emerged calling for equality and racial justice. These voices are strong and their determination is sure. All across America these new voices are demanding change and for this change to come to our nation swiftly.

Today, because of the growing masses of the disenfranchised and the dissatisfied, the societal structures that have given sanctuary to systemic racism in our nation are beginning to fall down. Those structures are falling down not only under the weight of their own shoddy construction, but are being aided in their fall by a generation that refuses to take such gross injustice anymore. From college campuses to our neighbors next door, there is a new cry for justice.

As we celebrate these new voices and new movements for justice, we must never forget what gave fuel to our present struggle. This new cry has arisen from the blood of new martyrs — men, women, boys, and girls — who died unnecessary deaths, whose names have been added to racism's enormous body count. Their blood still cries for justice even as Abel's blood cried out to the heavens when he was felled by his brother Cain.

This is a special and revolutionary time to be alive in America. From Confederate flags to historically inaccurate textbooks that conspire to cover up America's sins, it is all falling down. What is most critical in this hour is not just that these troubling hegemonies of injustice continue to be toppled, but that we erect something more just in their place.

In the Book of Nehemiah, the walls surrounding Jerusalem had been razed. Once a great nation, Israel had forgotten about the God who liberated them from their oppressors. Israel failed to live fully into God's divine imperative that they love all, both neighbor and stranger, as themselves. In their failures, Israel oppressed the weak, denied justice in their courts, and spilt the blood of innocents in the streets. As a result, it all fell down and Israel was forced into exile.

At a later time, as the prophet Nehemiah began to rebuild the wall, there were threats made against him by those who would not benefit from a stronger and more unified people in the land. Disturbingly, these threats remain present with us today, for there are many enemies of progress who have long benefited from our nation's maladies. Still, in this great and glorious hour, we are witnessing time and time again the power of a unified people strengthened and organized in pursuit of a just and noble cause.

So let the structures of racism in our nation continue to fall, and fall swiftly. Let us ready ourselves to build the foundations of a new America, a more just and beautiful America. Out of our painful past, let us finally build together an America where liberty and justice for all is more than just a pledge, but is our shared reality.

On Hills, Hope, and New Hearts:
A View from Dallas

When I saw the look in my wife's eyes, I knew something was terribly wrong.

Two days prior, I had received a call from Dr. Jeff Hood. His call went straight to my voicemail. When I saw his message pending, I already knew the reason for his call. The previous night, I had stayed up with my wife until the early hours of the morning, vexed by a video recording made viral on social media. The video depicted the final moments of Alton Sterling as he was fatally shot at point blank range by police officers in Baton Rouge. We watched the video again and again, seeking a sign that would justify the brutality we had just witnessed. We could find none.

Dr. Hood's call was not unusual or unexpected. Unfortunately, he had planned many solidarity rallies in response to acts of police brutality in recent years. We had previously stood together to speak out against this injustice.

I returned his call and we spoke. It was clear he was not expecting a large crowd, maybe 40 or 50 people. He believed there needed to be a show of solidarity in Dallas so that the people of Baton Rouge would not feel as though they were standing alone. I agreed and accepted his invitation to speak. I anticipated this would be my final public speaking appearance before heading to Philadelphia to join the 200th anniversary celebration of the African Methodist Episcopal Church already in progress.

However, the next evening, my wife and I again found ourselves viewing yet another gruesome act of brutality. This time, the location was the State of Minnesota. This time, the victim was Philando Castile. This time, the brutality was not just recorded but live-streamed to the world by his girlfriend. It was all too much to bear. Twice, and in as many days, all we could do was watch as another young Black man took his final breath, mortally wounded without just cause by the police.

My wife and I were not the only ones deeply moved by these acts of brutality. When we arrived that Thursday evening to the Belo Garden Park in Downtown Dallas, hundreds, not dozens, of people had already gathered. As the rally began, the evening's speakers and organizers ascended a small hill that provided a moving vantage point of the crowd. As I perused our large assembly, I was inspired by a picture of America: Black, White, Latino, Asian, Christian, Muslim, Jewish, middle-aged, Millennial, and children all standing side by side in 90-degree heat to declare that enough is enough.

After the rally, we marched together through the streets of downtown Dallas. Our great multitude made for a mighty witness against the scourge of police brutality. As we marched, Dallas police officers walked with us, guiding our route, directing traffic, ensuring our safety.

We made a final stop at the Old Red Courthouse as the march reached its conclusion. It was requested that I come forward and address the multitude and tell them about the brutality that had unfolded there in 1910 when a Black man was apprehended by a lynch mob, thrown out a second floor window, and dragged half a mile by a noose around his neck to the corner of Main and Akard Streets. There he was hung before an estimated crowd of 4000. I told the multitude that Dallas has a long legacy of hate, but that we were the generation that would make a difference. To this declaration the multitude roared its approval. I then invited everyone present to take a moment of silence for the many martyrs lost to police brutality.

Our moment of silence was the final act of our gathering. Instructions were then given for how to proceed from the courthouse back down Commerce Street to the originating point of the rally. The multitude began to disperse and to walk casually in the direction of their vehicles.

After walking with them for a moment, I stepped to the side to ensure everyone was proceeding forward. As I stood there, I felt an overwhelming sense of pride. We had gathered together under the pretense of great and seemingly unyielding pain, but the liturgy of our peaceful demonstration had provided many some needed release. Individuals walked over and greeted me, thanking me for the words I shared that evening.

My wife and a member of my ministerial staff were walking together in the crowd. I invited them over, thinking it best to stay together and not to have to find each other later amid the crowd. We needed to depart soon anyway to pick up our children from their weekly dance practice at the church. I also saw Imam Omar Suleiman, a friend and brother beside whom I had stood at seemingly countless vigils and rallies over the past year addressing everything from ending gun violence to stopping Islamophobia. I invited him to come over and stand with me as well. I also wanted to know his thoughts on the evening as a whole.

I took a brief glance back in the direction of the courthouse as the crowd continued to proceed down the road. A sudden movement caught my eye peripherally. I quickly turned my head to see a mass of humanity sprinting in my direction. When I saw the look in my wife's eyes, I knew something was terribly wrong.

Instinctively, I sprinted with the multitude. I, my wife, and others in our immediate area took shelter behind columns at the George Allen Courthouse. It was then that I heard rapid gunfire amid screams and sirens. I could not tell who was shooting, how many were shooting, or at whom they were shooting. I only knew that peace had been exchanged for sounds of war.

Against my wife's wishes, I lifted my head from behind the pillar. I needed to see. I did not want to be a sitting duck if gunmen were advancing in our direction. I did not see anyone immediately headed our way, and when I looked to my right, I saw a clear path. I encouraged everyone to run and not to stop running until we made it several blocks to the Omni Hotel.

That following Tuesday, I sat in the symphony center choir loft just behind the main stage as President Barack Obama addressed the nation. Four white police officers and one Latino police officer had been slain that fateful Thursday night by a lone Black gunman. Seven other officers were also wounded as well as two civilians. According to police, the gunman stated that he had come explicitly to kill white police officers. Still, I considered his crimes as crimes against us all, crimes against humanity, the same as I felt for the crimes that had first brought us together that evening.

From my exalted seat facing the audience, I watched as some of the wounded and recovering courageously entered the room amid tremendous applause. I also witnessed the endless tears that flowed from the fallen's family members as they sat in the first few rows. I could not take my eyes off one elderly father of one of the fallen, who wept for almost the entirety of the service. My heart broke for him. Still, I also saw strength in the sea of officers that had come to pay their respects.

The last several days had been a whirlwind for all of us. Still struggling to grasp the sudden tragedy that had unfolded that night, I was thrust into fulfilling media requests coming in constantly via phone, email, and social media from international, national, and local outlets. I stayed awake for almost 46 hours and canceled my travel to Philadelphia. There was no way that I could leave my city now. The memorial service provided me with my first opportunity just to sit and reflect.

As the President spoke, he commiserated about having to speak at far too many memorials following mass shooting tragedies over the course of his presidency. He shared that he sometimes struggled with the thought of whether or not Americans would ever find the character to open their hearts to each other and witness their "common humanity" and "shared dignity." Then President Obama offered inspiration from the pages of Scripture. He said, "I am reminded of what the Lord tells Ezekiel. 'I will give you a new heart,' the Lord says, 'and put a new spirit in you. I will remove from you your heart of stone, and give you a heart of flesh.' That's what we must pray for, each of us. A new heart. Not a heart of stone, but a heart open to the fears and hopes and challenges of our fellow citizens."

The President's words were profound. Undoubtedly, the racial hatred that has marred our nation is largely a matter of the heart.

Only with new hearts — hearts enlightened and transformed by the loving hand of God — can our nation be united as one. Only with new hearts will we be able to see ourselves, not just as Americans, but as part of the human family. Only with new hearts will we see, as Martin Luther King, Jr. so powerfully stated, that "We are caught in an inescapable network of mutuality, tied in a single garment of destiny. Whatever affects one directly, affects all indirectly."

That Thursday, exactly one week after the tragedy, I stood before a crowd assembled together in the newly minted chapel of the newly constructed Dallas County Parkland Hospital. I had previously been afforded the opportunity of speaking at the dedication of that chapel, and for the hospital's annual Martin Luther King, Jr. Celebration after that. This time, I was here to provide words of strength and comfort at a service of reflection and hope. Parkland had received seven of the wounded officers that fateful Thursday, and doctors there pronounced dead the first two officers they received. A palpable pain was easy to feel in the hospital.

In seeking to offer words of hope and encouragement to all who had assembled, and to many others watching the service being streamed throughout the hospital, I searched myself deeply in order to find that which brought me hope in the wake of the tragedy. As I searched within, I envisioned myself standing again upon the hill looking upon the multitude that had gathered for justice.

Once I found my hope, I spoke my hope. I said, "As we reflect upon all that has transpired in our city in recent days, as we reflect upon all that has transpired in this hospital in recent days, what hope can we find to sustain us and strengthen us for the road ahead? I must admit that at times like these, in the midst of these tensions, hope is sometimes hard to locate. However, here is the hope that I have found. While one person caused great pain last Thursday, he was greatly outnumbered. My hope rests in my confidence that there are more of us than of him, both in the world and in this hospital, persons committed to the preservation of life, yes even at the sacrifice and lying down of their own. And our commitment to the preservation of life remains. Dare I say that because of tragedy our commitment has been made stronger?"

Amid the difficulties and disappointments that accompany our present struggle for justice, hope sometimes seems fleeting. At times, long-fought victories may seem suddenly shattered. In the midst of the struggle, it can be easy to lose heart.

During times of overwhelming pain and unyielding struggle, yes, even times such as these, it proves essential to change one's vantage point. Climb high upon the hill. Climb high upon the hill for a clear view. For upon the hill, we see that far more stand for the cause of peace and justice than those who seek to cause humanity harm. Upon the hill, our hope is made sure and our hearts are made new. Upon the hill, we bear witness to a picture of Heaven while still standing upon the earth, those of every nation and tongue who shall one day gather before the throne of God.

May we forever look to the hills, hold on to our hope, and seek new hearts. May the brutalities that separate us give way to the bonds of humanity that makes us one. And may we continue to pursue justice until "justice flows like waters and righteousness like a mighty stream."

Notes

[1]Brian K. Blount, ed., *True to Our Native Land: An African American Bible Commentary* (Minneapolis: Fortress Press, 2007), 559.

[2]De La Soul, "Stakes Is High, *Stakes Is High*," Tommy Boy Entertainment, 1996.

[3]Toby Harnden, "Barack Obama faces 30 death threats a day, stretching US Secret Service," *The Telegraph*, August 3, 2009.

[4]Juliet Eilperin, "The new dynamics of protecting a president: Most threats against Obama issued online," *The Washington Post*, October 8, 2014.

[5]Emma Green, "The Evangelical Reckoning Over Donald Trump," *The Atlantic*, November 10, 2016.

[6]Philip Bump, "Trump got the most GOP votes ever — both for and against him — and other fun facts," *The Washington Post*, June 8, 2016.

[7]Kate Shellnutt, "Trump Elected President, Thanks to 4 in 5 White Evangelicals," *Christianity Today*, November 9, 2016.

[8]Michael Finnegan and Noah Bierman, "Trump's endorsement of violence reaches new level: He may pay legal fees for assault suspect," *Los Angeles Times*, March 13, 2016.

[9]Lisa Mascaro, "David Duke and other white supremacists see Trump's rise as way to increase role in mainstream politics," *Los Angeles Times*, September 29, 2016.

[10]Lauren McGaughy, "White nationalist who led "Hail Trump' chant to speak at Texas A&M, though school didn't invite him," *Dallas Morning News,* November 23, 2016.

[11]Southern Poverty Law Center, "Ten Days After: Harassment and Intimidation in the Aftermath of the Election," November 29, 2016.

[12]Teryn Payne, "Gun Sales Among Blacks See Increase," *Ebony Magazine*, November 29, 2016.

[13]Malcolm X, excerpt from remarks delivered on May 5, 1962 at the funeral service of Ronald Stokes in Los Angeles, California. Mr. Stokes was killed by the Los Angeles Police Department.

[14]Muhammad Ali released his statement to news outlets in December 2015, when Donald Trump first floated the idea of banning all Muslim immigration. See nbcnews.com/news/us-news/muhammad-ali-hits-trump-misguided-murderers-sabotaging-islam-n477351 .

[15]Martin Luther King, Jr., excerpt from speech entitled "The Other America," delivered March 14, 1968 at Grosse Pointe High School in Grosse Pointe, Michigan, http://www.gphistorical.org/mlk/mlkspeech/.

[16]Martin Luther King, Jr., excerpt from Nobel Lecture entitled "The Quest for Peace and Justice," delivered on December 11, 1964 at the University of Oslo in Oslo, Norway, http://www.nobelprize.org/nobel_prizes/peace/laureates/1964/king-lecture.html .

[17]Martin Luther King, Jr., "Letter from a Birmingham Jail" (April 16, 1963), https://www.africa.upenn.edu/Articles_Gen/Letter_Birmingham.html.

[18]Robert P. Hay, "And Ten Dollars Extra, for Every Hundred Lashes Any Person Will Give Him, to the Amount of Three Hundred": A Note on Andrew Jackson's Runaway Slave Ad of 1804 and on the Historian's Use of Evidence," *Tennessee Historical Quarterly,* vol. 36, no. 4 (WINTER 1977), 468–78.

[19]Carmen DeNavas-Wait, Bernadette D. Proctor, Jessica C. Smith, "Income, Poverty, and Health Insurance Coverage in the United States: 2009," *Current Population Reports,* U.S. Census Bureau, 15.

[20]Aaron Morrison, "Black Unemployment Rate 2015: In Better Economy, African-Americans See Minimal Gains," *I.B. Times,* March 8, 2015.

[21]Jonnelle Marte, "The economy's troubling double standard for Black men," *The Washington Post,* July 2, 2014.

[22]Rakesh Kochhar and Richard Fry, "Wealth inequality has widened along racial, ethnic lines since end of Great Recession," Pew Research Center, December 12, 2014.

[23]Barack Obama, "Statement on the Grand Jury Decision in the Death of Eric Garner," delivered December 2, 2014, at The White House, Washington, D.C., https://www.whitehouse.gov/blog/2014/12/03/president-obama-delivers-statement-grand-jury-decision-death-eric-garner.

[24]Joerg Rieger, *Christ and Empire: From Paul to Postcolonial Times* (Minneapolis: Fortress Press, 2007), 2–3.

[25]Martin Luther King, Jr., Excerpt from Nobel Lecture.

ABOUT THE AUTHOR

The Reverend Dr. Michael W. Waters is founder and Senior Pastor of Joy Tabernacle A.M.E. Church in Dallas, Texas, one of the fastest-growing A.M.E. churches in the state, and the newly appointed Senior Pastor of the nearly 100-year-old Agape Temple A.M.E. Church in Dallas, Texas. The two congregations now operate under one vision and one pastoral leader as the congregations unite together as one Joy Tabernacle. As pastor, professor, author, social commentator, and community leader, Dr. Waters's words of hope and empowerment inspire national and international audiences. He has been featured, mentioned, profiled, and quoted upon such esteemed platforms as ABC's *Nightline,* The Associated Press, BBC's *Newsnight,* Bill Moyers, *CBS This Morning, The Christian Century, Ebony Magazine, GQ Magazine,* HufffPost Live, MSNBC, National Public Radio, *NBC Nightly News, PBS Newshour,* HBO'S *VICE,* and *The Washington Post.*

Dr. Waters holds bachelor, master, and doctoral degree with honors from Southern Methodist University and the SMU Perkins School of Theology in Dallas, Texas, where he also serves as an adjunct professor in the Doctor of Ministry Degree Program, as North Texas Peer Preaching Group Facilitator in the Perkins Center for Preaching Excellence, and as a member of the Perkins Executive Board. He is the award-winning author of *Freestyle: Reflections on Faith, Family, Justice, and Pop Culture* (Upper Room Books, 2014).

Dr. Waters was named "2016 Community Leader of the Year" by the Council on American-Islamic Relations, "Pastor of the Year" at the Center for Theological Activism's 2015 Justice Awards, and he was listed among the *Dallas Business Journal's* "40 Under 40" Class of 2015. Dr. Waters is also a recipient of Southern Methodist University's Distinguished Alumni Emerging Leader Award presented to "an emerging leader in a particular discipline, organization, or cause that has brought distinction to the University." Among numerous boards and commissions, Dr. Waters serves as the Dallas City Council-appointed chair of the Martin Luther King, Jr. Community Center—which offers comprehensive social services and cultural and educational opportunities to over 300,000 Dallas citizens annually—and as inaugural Co-Chair of Faith Forward Dallas, an initiative of the Thanks-Giving Square Foundation, recently awarded a Global Goals Award by the United Nations Association for its work in peace and justice.

Married to Mrs. Yulise Reaves Waters, Esq., Dr. and Atty. Waters are the proud parents of three children: Michael Jeremiah, Hope Yulise, and Liberty Grace. The family resides in the historic South Dallas community of Dallas, Texas.